CHURCHIANITY: HOW MODERN AMERICAN CHURCHES CORRUPTED GENERATIONS OF CHRISTIANS

JONATHAN DEL ARROZ

FOREWORD

CHURCHIANITY: THE GREAT APOSTASY

The modern Church in the West stands at a crossroads, though many of its congregants appear blissfully unaware that they have already chosen a wide and easy path to Hell. What passes for Christianity in the twenty-first century would be unrecognizable to the Church Fathers, incomprehensible to the medieval scholastics, and abhorrent to the Reformers. We are witnessing nothing less than the attempted replacement of Christianity with its heretical doppelganger: Churchianity.

Churchianity is the systematic subordination of Christian doctrine to the prevailing ideology of social justice. It is the elevation of worldly concerns above spiritual ones, the replacement of timeless Biblical authority with the dynamic mainstream Narrative, and the transformation of the Church from a beacon of eternal truth into an echo chamber for Earthly politics. Most damning of all, it represents the complete inversion of Christianity's fundamental premise: instead of being in the world but not of it, Churchianity insists on being entirely of the world while maintaining an increasingly unconvincing veneer of theological legitimacy.

Churchianity is not just another in the long line of traditional doctrinal disputes. This is apostasy wearing a clerical collar, heresy draped in liturgical vestments, and blasphemy proclaimed from ten thousand pulpits every Sunday morning. The tragedy is not that wolves have entered the sheepfold—Jesus Christ himself warned us they would come. The tragedy is that the sheep now bleat in self-righteous pride as they are led astray by those who seek to destroy them.

At its core, Churchianity represents a fundamental misunderstanding of the nature of both God and man. Whereas Christianity proclaims the fallen nature of humanity and the absolute necessity of divine redemption, Churchianity preaches the perfectibility of man through political correctness. Whereas Christianity promises the Kingdom of Heaven, Churchianity prioritizes earthly justice. And whereas Christianity demands repentance from sin, Churchianity demands repentance for a whole host of invented man-made sins, including failure to adequately genuflect before whatever victim class currently sits atop the intersectional hierarchy.

The mechanism of this theological perversion is breathtakingly simple: take any Biblical command, strip it of its soteriological context, and reinterpret it through the lens of contemporary social justice politics. "Love thy neighbor" ceases to be about individual charity and becomes a mandate for open borders and mass immigration. "Care for the poor" transforms from personal almsgiving into advocacy for higher taxes, foreign wars, and welfare states. "Welcome the stranger" transforms from basic hospitality into a divine command to facilitate the demographic replacement of the nation.

This hermeneutical vandalism not only does violence to individual verses, but to the entire Biblical narrative. The God who destroyed Sodom and Gomorrah, who commanded the Israelites to maintain their distinctiveness among the nations, who confused the languages at Babel to create the nations—this God is reimagined as a cosmic social worker whose primary concern is ensuring equal outcomes across all demographic categories. The savior who said "My kingdom is not of this world" is recast as a proto-hippie community organizer whose death was not intended to atone for personal sins, but for 17th-century colonization.

No Christian Church has shown itself to be completely immune to this subversive contagion. The Roman Catholic Church, which for centuries stood as a bulwark against heresy, now finds itself led by clerics who are more concerned about climate change than for the salvation of men's souls. The current occupant of Peter's throne speaks more passionately about carbon emissions than abortion, more forcefully about income inequality than sexual morality, and far more frequently about migrants than martyrs. The Church that once launched the Crusades to defend Christendom now declares it a moral imperative to welcome to the West those who would see every cross destroyed and every cathedral burned to the ground.

The Anglican Communion, already weakened by its centuries of compromise with secular authority, has completed its transformation into the Conservative Party at prayer—if the Conservative Party were still conservative and one could find a Tory who was not Hindu, Muslim, or Jewish. Canterbury's pronouncements are all-but-indistinguishable from *Guardian* editorials, complete with the requisite hand-wringing about colonialism, slavery, and the urgent need to make monetary reparations for crimes committed by people long dead to people who were never wronged.

The mainline Protestant denominations have fared even worse. The Lutherans who once thundered "Here I stand" now whimper "Here I kneel"—before every fashionable cause and politically correct crusade. The Methodists, Presbyterians, and Episcopalians compete to see who can more thoroughly repudiate their theological heritage in favor of sexual perversion, rainbow flags and moral relativism. These churches have hemorrhaged members in recent decades, not because Christianity is dying, but because Churchianity offers nothing that cannot be found in a political party or a gay disco.

Even the evangelical churches, which initially resisted this insidious corruption, have begun to succumb. Megachurch pastors discover that sermon series on "social justice" fill more seats than expositions of Romans. Youth pastors find that endorsing movements like Black Lives Matter provides them with more social cachet than leading Bible studies. Entire denominations that once prioritized evangelism now prioritize "racial reconciliation," which in practice means white self-flagellation and endless apologies for nonexistent sins neither committed nor inherited.

Jesus Christ told us we would know them by their fruits, and the fruits of Churchianity are bitter indeed. Churches that embrace this heresy invariably experience the same progression: first comes the theological compromise, then the demographic decline, and finally the institutional death. The pattern is as predictable as it is pathetic.

Initially, the leadership declares that Christianity must evolve in order to remain relevant. Traditional doctrines are either quietly abandoned or radically reinterpreted. Sexual morality is usually first casualty—after all, nothing says "love" like affirming sexual deviants in their sin. The authority of Scripture is undermined through appeals to sympathy, cultural contexts and societal progress. The exclusivity of the salvation offered by Jesus Christ is downplayed in favor of a luke-warm universalism intended to avoid any risk of offending sinners and nonbelievers.

Next comes the exodus of believers who recognize apostasy when they see it, even if they are unwilling to openly call it out. Families that have attended the same church for generations quietly slip away. The youth, offered nothing but the same social justice they get at school, see no reason to wake up early on Sunday morning for a sixth dose of the weekly propaganda. The pews empty, the offering plates remain unfilled, and the Churchian leadership inevitably responds by doubling down on their failed strategy.

Finally comes the death rattle. The beautiful historic building is sold to developers who convert it into restaurants, mosques, and even night clubs. The congregation, now consisting of a few dozen elderly regulars, merges with another dying church to forestall the inevitable for a few more years. And the denomination's bureaucracy soldiers on, issuing increasingly irrelevant statements about racism and refugees to an audience that consists primarily of other bureaucrats.

This is not speculation or hyperbole. This is the documented history of virtually every church body that has embraced Churchianity. The Episcopal Church in America has lost more than half its membership since embracing social justice theology. The United Church of Christ has declined by two-thirds. The Presbyterian Church continues its death spiral, closing churches at a rate that would constitute a crisis if anyone still cared enough to notice. Even the once-staunch Southern Baptist is in decline, having lost 21 percent of its membership since 2001.

Churchianity is not just a weakened or compromised form of Christianity. It is actively anti-Christian. It does not merely fail to proclaim the Gospel; it proclaims an anti-Gospel of inverted Christianity. Where Christianity offers salvation from sin, Churchianity offers affirmation of sin. Where Christianity demands transformation, Churchianity demands tolerance. Where Christianity proclaims objective truth, Churchianity preaches subjective experience.

This anti-Christian essence reveals itself most clearly in Churchianity's relationship with actual Bible-believing Christians. Orthodox believers who maintain traditional positions on marriage, sexuality, and the exclusivity of Christ are not met with disagreement and debate, they are demonized. They are called bigots, haters, and racists. They are excluded from fellowship, driven from denominations, and subjected to ecclesiastical trials that would make the Spanish Inquisition blush. The one unforgivable sin in Churchianity is believing what Christians have always believed.

At the same time, those who actively oppose Christianity are welcomed with open arms. Islamic prayers are offered in ostensibly Christian churches. Atheist activists are invited to lecture congregations about their moral failings. Pagan practices are incorporated into worship services in the name of "inclusivity." The Church that once conquered the Roman Empire through martyrdom now conquers itself through suicide.

Churchianity represents the greatest threat to Christianity since the rise of Islam. It is far more dangerous to the Church than external persecution because it corrupts from within. It is more deadly than direct intellectual assault because it operates through insidious rhetoric and emotional manipulation. And it is more effective than most previous heresies because it speaks the language of the Church while inverting and subverting the actual teachings of Christ.

But truth remains truth regardless of how many deny it. The Gospel remains the Gospel regardless of how many pervert it. Jesus Christ remains the Lord and Savior of Mankind no matter how many betray Him. And the gates of Hell, whether they take the form of Roman persecution, Islamic invasion, or Churchian subversion, shall never prevail.

The question for every reader of this book is straighforward: Where do you stand? Do you stand with the apostles and the martyrs, the reformers and the revivalists, and with the faithful remnant throughout history who have refused to bow the knee to false gods? Or will you worship a fake social justice Jesus in a false church with those who have sold their souls for fame, fortune, and worldly approval?

Now, brethren, concerning the coming of our Lord Jesus Christ and our gathering together to Him, we ask you, not to be soon shaken in mind or troubled, either by spirit or by word or by letter, as if from us, as though the day of Christ had come. Let no one deceive you by any means; for that Day will not come unless the falling away comes first...

2 Thessalonians 2: 1-3

Vox Day
21 August 2025

INTRODUCTION: THE GREAT DECEPTION

I walked into church on a Sunday morning in 2020, expecting to hear the Gospel of Jesus Christ. Instead, I got a lecture on social justice.

For decades, I had been a faithful member of my local American church. I volunteered 12 to 20 hours a week as the keyboardist in their contemporary worship band. I watched as they ripped out the traditional pews and replaced them with chairs, installed smoke machines and concert lighting, and transformed Sunday service into something resembling a TED Talk more than worship. The pastor wore Air Jordans to the pulpit and spent more time talking about his family vacations than the Word of God.

But nothing prepared me for what came next.

As the pandemic shutdowns began, our church moved online. Suddenly freed from the constraints of face-to-face accountability, the messages became increasingly political. The pastor began preaching about "white privilege" and "systemic racism." He recommended books like "White Fragility" from the pulpit. During the height of the Black Lives Matter riots, he took a knee for his Instagram account, turning the message of Christ into a photo opportunity for social media virtue signaling.

When I tried to raise concerns about these departures from

biblical teaching, I was told the pastor was too busy to meet with me. Instead, they sent me to speak with a woman who handled adminis- trative duties - a woman who, I discovered, was functioning as a pastor despite the clear biblical prohibition in 1 Timothy 2:12: "But I do not allow a woman to teach or exercise authority over a man, but to remain quiet."

The message was unmistakable: if you wanted deep relationships with Christ and to maintain biblical tradition, you wouldn't be welcome here.

I wrote a detailed letter of admonishment to the church leader- ship, carefully documenting the theological problems I had witnessed and providing scriptural support for my concerns. The response was silence. No discussion. No biblical defense of their positions. No will- ingness to engage with Scripture. They simply ignored the letter and continued down their path of compromise.

That's when I realized I wasn't dealing with real Christianity anymore. I was dealing with something else entirely, something I now call "Churchianity."

The Cancer of Compromise

What I experienced wasn't unique to my church. Across America, churches have abandoned the Gospel of Jesus Christ in favor of a consumer-friendly product designed to attract crowds and avoid offense. They've traded the narrow gate that leads to life for the broad road that leads to destruction, exactly as Christ warned in Matthew 7:13-14: "Enter through the narrow gate. For wide is the gate and broad is the road that leads to destruction, and many enter through it. But small is the gate and narrow the road that leads to life, and only a few find it."

Modern American Churchianity has become infected with social justice cancer, a malignant ideology that starts small but metastasizes until it completely destroys the church's purpose: proclaiming the good news that Jesus Christ's sacrifice and resurrection absolved all sins for those who believe.

When churches begin prioritizing social causes over salvation, entertainment over worship, and cultural acceptance over biblical truth, they cease to be churches in any meaningful sense. They become social clubs with religious decorations, community centers with Christian branding, or worse, propaganda outlets using the name of Christ to advance worldly agendas.

The statistics tell the story. Church attendance has plummeted in these places and younger generations are flocking back to more traditional Catholic and Orthodox churches to get something that is more in line with what their ancestors believed. Biblical literacy has collapsed. But instead of returning to the Word of God, most American churches have doubled down on their compromise, convinced that being more like the world will somehow win the world.

They've forgotten Christ's own words in John 15:19: "If you belonged to the world, it would love you as its own. As it is, you do not belong to the world, but I have chosen you out of the world. That is why the world hates you."

The Deception Runs Deep

The tragedy isn't just that these churches have abandoned biblical Christianity, but they've also convinced millions of Americans that their corrupted version IS biblical Christianity. Entire generations have grown up thinking that Christianity is about social activism, therapeutic self-help, and material prosperity rather than repentance, holiness, and eternal salvation.

They've created what I call "Churchianity," a counterfeit faith that uses Christian vocabulary while promoting anti-Christian values. It looks like Christianity from the outside, but it's hollow at the core. It promises everything the world wants to hear while avoiding everything the world needs to hear.

This Churchianity tells people they're basically good and just need to embrace their authentic selves. Biblical Christianity teaches that we're sinners in desperate need of a Savior. Churchianity promises health, wealth, and happiness in this life. Biblical Christianity promises persecution, suffering, and eternal joy in the next. Churchianity seeks to be relevant to the culture. Biblical Christianity seeks to transform the culture through the power of the Gospel.

The difference isn't subtle. It's the difference between truth and lies, between salvation and damnation, between the narrow gate and the broad road.

What This Book Will Expose

In the pages that follow, I'm going to show you exactly how American churches have been corrupted and what you can do to protect yourself and your family from this deception. This isn't an academic exercise. This is spiritual warfare, and souls are at stake.

First, we'll examine the cancer itself - how social justice ideology infiltrated American churches and why Christians proved so susceptible to its lies. You'll learn the history of this movement, its Marxist roots, and the specific tactics used to manipulate Christian conscience into supporting anti-Christian causes.

Then we'll identify the warning signs. I've developed a list of six clear indicators that a church has been compromised by social justice ideology. If your church exhibits even one of these signs, you need to take action immediately. If it exhibits multiple signs, you need to leave before the spiritual damage spreads to your family.

We'll explore the modern obsession with "online church" and digital ministry - why virtual fellowship isn't fellowship at all and how the entertainment complex has replaced authentic worship. You'll see how churches have adopted corporate marketing strategies, treating congregants like consumers rather than souls in need of salvation.

One of the most devastating losses in Christianity has been the abandonment of sacramental life. We'll examine what the Reformation threw away in its zeal to reform the Catholic Church, and why the Catholic and Orthodox Churches' preservation of sacred tradition offers lessons that modern Christians desperately need to learn.

We'll confront the uncomfortable truth about sin and purity that modern churches refuse to address. The prosperity gospel has poisoned American Christianity with false promises of health and wealth, while churches avoid preaching about the sins that are destroying our culture: sexual immorality, abortion, materialism, and pride. Christ himself warned that it's easier for a camel to go through the eye of a needle than for a rich man to enter the kingdom of God (Matthew 19:24), yet American churches preach a gospel of material blessing that would make Christ himself unwelcome in their sanctuaries.

The Personal Cost of Truth

I want to be clear about something from the beginning: this book will cost you. If you take its message seriously, you may have to leave your church. You may lose friends. Your family might think you've become a religious extremist. The comfortable Christianity you've known may be revealed as a lie, and the truth may be harder to live than the deception.

But the alternative is worse. The alternative is watching your children grow up believing lies about God. The alternative is spending your life in a spiritual wasteland, thinking you're following Christ while actually following the world. The alternative is discovering on judgment day that your "Christianity" was actually Churchianity, and that you never knew the real Jesus at all.

Christ himself warned us about this in Matthew 7:21-23: "Not everyone who says to me, 'Lord, Lord,' will enter the kingdom of heaven, but only the one who does the will of my Father who is in heaven. Many will say to me on that day, 'Lord, Lord, did we not prophesy in your name and in your name drive out demons and in your name perform many miracles?' Then I will tell them plainly, 'I never knew you. Away from me, you evildoers!'"

How many people sitting in American churches today think they know Jesus, but Jesus doesn't know them? How many have been deceived by a false gospel that promises salvation without repentance, blessing without obedience, and heaven without holiness?

The Remnant Remains

I know it's sounded like doom and gloom so far, but there is hope. Throughout history, God has preserved a remnant of faithful believers even in the darkest times. There are still churches that preach the whole counsel of God. There are still pastors who fear God

11

more than they fear man. There are still Christians who choose the narrow gate despite its difficulty.

This book will help you find them. More importantly, it will help you become one of them.

The great deception of our time is that Christianity should be easy, popular, and comfortable. The truth is that following Christ has always been difficult, unpopular, and costly. Christ himself said in Luke 9:23: "Whoever wants to be my disciple must deny themselves and take up their cross daily and follow me."

Modern Churchianity has removed the cross. It preaches a Christianity without sacrifice, discipleship without discipline, and salvation without surrender. It's not Christianity at all.

The Choice Before Us

You have a choice to make. You can continue in the comfortable deception of modern American Christianity, attending churches that tell you what you want to hear while avoiding what you need to hear. You can keep pretending that entertainment is worship, that social activism is evangelism, and that feeling good about yourself is the same as being right with God.

Or you can choose the difficult path of biblical Christianity. You can seek out churches that preach the whole Word of God, even when it's uncomfortable. You can embrace the narrow gate that leads to life, even though few find it. You can take up your cross daily and follow Christ, even when the world - and other "Christians" - hate you for it.

The stakes couldn't be higher. This isn't about denominational preferences or worship styles. This is about the Gospel itself. This is about whether American Christianity will return to its biblical roots or continue its slide into irrelevant apostasy.

This is about whether you and your family will follow Christ or follow the crowd.

The choice is yours. But choose carefully, because eternity hangs in the balance.

1

THE CANCER SPREADS -
OVERVIEW OF THE PROBLEM

THE NUMBERS DON'T LIE, EVEN WHEN THE CHURCHES DO.

In 1973, churches commanded the respect and attention of over 60% of Americans. Mainline denominations alone (Methodist, Lutheran, Presbyterian, Episcopal) accounted for 55% of all Protestants. These were the backbone of American society, shaping culture, influencing politics, and providing moral guidance to entire communities.

Today, that number has collapsed to roughly 40% of the population, with mainline churches representing 29% of Protestants. The pews are emptying, the offering plates are lighter, and an entire generation has walked away from organized religion entirely. Church leaders scratch their heads and wonder what went wrong, but the answer is staring them in the face every Sunday morning.

They abandoned Christianity for something else entirely.

The Great Transformation

Walk into most American churches fifty years ago, and you'd find something radically different from today's entertainment complexes. Services followed traditional liturgical patterns that had been refined over centuries. Congregations sang hymns that connected them to believers across history and around the world. Sermons focused on doctrinal teaching, biblical exposition, and moral instruction rooted in Scripture.

The church building itself reflected the sacred nature of worship. Pews faced forward toward the altar, emphasizing that worship was directed toward God, not toward entertaining the congregation. Stained glass windows told biblical stories. The architecture itself proclaimed that this was a holy place, set apart from the ordinary world.

Most importantly, these churches understood their primary mission: proclaiming the Gospel of Jesus Christ for the salvation of souls. Everything else, social programs, community events, even charitable work, flowed from that central purpose. The church existed to make disciples, not to make people feel good about themselves.

Compare that to what passes for worship today. Churches have ripped out their pews and installed theater seating. They've removed crosses and stained glass in favor of video screens and concert lighting. The "sanctuary" has become an "auditorium," and the "congregation" has become an "audience."

The pastor, who often now prefers to be called a "teaching pastor" or "lead communicator," takes the stage in designer jeans and expensive sneakers. His sermon is a motivational speech peppered with pop psychology, personal anecdotes, and carefully selected Bible verses taken out of context. The goal isn't to challenge the audience with biblical truth but to make them feel inspired and entertained.

This isn't evolution. This is revolution. And it's destroying American Christianity from within.

The Consumer Church Model

The most devastating change in American Christianity has been the adoption of a consumer mentality. Churches now operate like businesses competing for market share, with congregants treated as customers whose needs must be met and whose preferences must be accommodated.

This consumer model has infected every aspect of church life. Worship services are designed based on focus group feedback and demographic studies. Sermons are crafted to avoid offense and maximize attendance. Church programs are evaluated based on participation numbers rather than spiritual fruit. Even the Gospel itself has been repackaged as a consumer product - "Jesus will make your life better" rather than "Repent and believe."

The results are predictable. When you treat people like consumers, they behave like consumers. They shop around for churches that offer the best programs, the most entertaining services, and the least demanding messages. They switch churches as easily as they switch brands of toothpaste. And when they get bored or find something better, they leave.

This consumer Christianity has produced a generation of believers who know nothing about sacrifice, commitment, or spiritual discipline. They've been taught that Christianity is about what God can do for them, not what they owe to God. They expect to be entertained, inspired, and affirmed, but they've never been taught to deny themselves, take up their cross, and follow Christ.

Christ himself warned against this mentality in Luke 9:23-24: "Whoever wants to be my disciple must deny themselves and take up their cross daily and follow me. For whoever wants to save their life will lose it, but whoever loses their life for me will save it."

Modern American Christianity has turned this upside down. Instead of losing your life for Christ, churches promise that Christ will improve your life. Instead of taking up your cross, they promise to remove your burdens. Instead of denying yourself, they encourage you to embrace your authentic self.

It's the opposite of Christianity, marketed under the Christian brand.

Personal Witness to the Decline

I watched this transformation happen in real time at my own church, well, in two churches. The first one I saw, but didn't recognize it as a pattern until I'd been to a second that went down the same path. What started as subtle changes, replacing hymns with contemporary music, casual dress for the pastor, and more personal stories in sermons, gradually accelerated into something unrecognizable.

The breaking point came during the late 2010s when our church brought in a member of the San Francisco 49ers to speak about Colin Kaepernick's kneeling during the national anthem. This football player stood in our pulpit and declared that Kaepernick's protest was "something from God," a divine calling to fight racial injustice.

I sat in that pew, stunned. Here was a man who barely knew Scripture, who had no theological training, who was being held up as a spiritual authority because he played professional sports. And he was using our pulpit to promote a political protest that had nothing to do with the Gospel and everything to do with one man's ego and career ambitions.

This was the beginning of a problem that repeated itself and amplified further across different denominations during the 2020 Black Lives Matter protests, as pastors tried to get behind the cool social justice movement on televisions and preach that the greatest of all sins was racism, a concept that wasn't even invented until the 20th century. Were they really saying Christianity was off base for nearly 2000 years? It appeared so.

The Prosperity Gospel Poison

While social justice ideology has infected many mainline churches, the prosperity gospel has poisoned evangelical and Pentecostal denominations with equal devastation. This heretical teaching promises that God wants all believers to be healthy, wealthy, and successful in this life - a direct contradiction of Christ's own words and example.

Jesus himself lived in poverty, warning his followers that "foxes have dens and birds have nests, but the Son of Man has no place to lay his head" (Matthew 8:20). He told the rich young ruler to sell everything and give to the poor (Matthew 19:21). He declared that it's easier for a camel to go through the eye of a needle than for a rich man to enter the kingdom of God (Matthew 19:24).

Yet prosperity preachers live in mansions, fly in private jets, and promise their followers that faith will bring material blessings. They twist Scripture to support their greed, turning the Gospel into a get-rich-quick scheme that would make Christ himself flip tables in righteous anger.

The damage goes beyond the obvious financial exploitation. The prosperity gospel teaches people to evaluate God's love based on their circumstances. When the promised health and wealth don't materialize, believers either blame themselves for lacking faith or abandon Christianity entirely.

This false gospel has produced a generation of Christians who know nothing about suffering, persecution, or the cost of discipleship. They've been taught that following Christ should make life easier, not harder. When they encounter the inevitable trials that come with living in a fallen world, they're spiritually unprepared and often shipwreck their faith.

The Entertainment Complex

Perhaps nowhere is the corruption of American Christianity more visible than in the rise of the mega-church entertainment complex. These massive operations, some drawing tens of thousands of attendees, have perfected the art of religious theater.

The "worship experience" begins in a parking lot managed by professional traffic coordinators. Greeters with headsets and clipboards direct visitors to information booths staffed by volunteers trained in customer service techniques. The lobby features coffee bars, bookstores, and interactive displays that wouldn't look out of place in a shopping mall.

The main auditorium rivals professional concert venues. Multi-million-dollar sound systems, theatrical lighting, fog machines, and massive video screens create an atmosphere designed to generate emotional responses rather than spiritual reverence.

The worship team, a carefully curated group of attractive, talented performers (and yes, I took part and am admonishing myself!), leads the audience through a set list of contemporary songs designed to build energy and create emotional peaks. The music is loud, repetitive, and focused on feelings rather than theological content. Many of the songs could be love songs to a romantic partner if you changed a few pronouns.

When the teaching pastor takes the stage, he's dressed like a successful businessman or trendy influencer. His message is a carefully crafted presentation complete with video clips, humorous anecdotes, and practical life advice. The goal isn't to expound Scripture but to deliver an inspiring talk that will keep people coming back next week.

This entire production requires enormous financial resources and professional staff. The church operates like a corporation, with marketing departments, brand managers, and customer retention strategies. Success is measured by attendance numbers, social media followers, and revenue growth rather than spiritual fruit or biblical faithfulness.

The "Preachers with Sneakers" Instagram account perfectly captures this phenomenon, documenting pastors who wear thousand-dollar shoes and designer clothing while preaching to congregations struggling with financial hardship. These men have turned the Gospel into a personal brand and the church into their platform for self-promotion.

Christ drove the money changers from the temple with a whip, declaring, "My house will be called a house of prayer, but you are making it a den of robbers" (Matthew 21:13). What would he do with pastors who've turned his house into a concert venue and his Gospel into a marketing campaign?

The Abandonment of Biblical Authority

Underlying all these corruptions is a fundamental rejection of biblical authority. Modern churches have embraced "cafeteria Christianity," picking and choosing which parts of Scripture to follow based on cultural acceptability rather than divine command.

Verses about sexual morality are dismissed as culturally outdated. Passages about church leadership are reinterpreted to accommodate feminist ideology. Warnings about false teachers are ignored when those teachers are popular or profitable. The clear teachings of Christ himself are subordinated to the opinions of secular psychologists, social activists, and marketing consultants.

This selective approach to Scripture destroys the foundation of Christian faith. If believers can dismiss any biblical teaching that makes them uncomfortable, then the Bible ceases to be the Word of

God and becomes merely the opinions of ancient men. If cultural trends determine which parts of Scripture are valid, then culture becomes the ultimate authority rather than God.

The Apostle Paul warned Timothy about this exact problem: "For the time will come when people will not put up with sound doctrine. Instead, to suit their own desires, they will gather around them a great number of teachers to say what their itching ears want to hear. They will turn their ears away from the truth and turn aside to myths" (2 Timothy 4:3-4).

That time has come. American churches are filled with people who want to hear that they're basically good, that God exists to serve their needs, and that following Christ requires no real sacrifice or change. They've found plenty of teachers willing to tell them exactly what they want to hear.

The Cost of Compromise

The real cost isn't in statsitics like engagement rates, but is measured in souls. Some people who think they're Christians but have never heard the real Gospel, families are destroyed by false teaching, and children are raised on spiritual junk food who lack the biblical foundation to withstand life's storms.

When churches abandon their primary mission of proclaiming the Gospel for the salvation of souls, they lose their reason for existence. They become social clubs with religious decorations, community centers with Christian branding, or entertainment venues with spiritual themes. They may attract crowds, generate revenue, and receive positive media coverage, but they're no longer churches in any biblical sense.

Christ warned that many would come to him on judgment day claiming to have prophesied, cast out demons, and performed miracles in his name, only to hear him say, "I never knew you. Away from me, you evildoers!" (Matthew 7:23). How many people sitting in American churches today fit this description? How many think they know Jesus, but Jesus doesn't know them?

The Path Forward

The corruption of American Christianity didn't happen overnight, and it won't be reversed quickly. But it can be reversed. Throughout history, God has raised up faithful men and women to call his people back to biblical truth. The Reformation itself began when one priest decided that Scripture mattered more than church tradition or popular opinion.

The first step is recognition. Christians must acknowledge that much of what passes for Christianity in America today is actually something else entirely. They must be willing to compare their churches, their pastors, and their own beliefs against the clear teaching of Scripture, regardless of how uncomfortable that comparison might be.

The second step is separation. Believers must be willing to leave churches that have abandoned biblical Christianity, even if those churches are popular, convenient, or socially acceptable. Christ called his followers to be in the world but not of the world, and that includes not being of the worldly church.

The third step is restoration. Christians must seek out churches that preach the whole counsel of God, practice biblical discipline, and prioritize the Gospel over entertainment, social causes, or financial success. These churches exist, but they're often small, unfashionable, and demanding.

The cancer has spread, but it hasn't won. The gates of hell will not prevail against Christ's true church, even if they've already conquered much of American Christianity. The question isn't whether faithful Christianity will survive - Christ has already guaranteed that. The question is whether you and your family will be part of the faithful remnant or part of the compromised majority.

2

THE TROJAN HORSE - SOCIAL JUSTICE HISTORY AND CHRISTIAN SUSCEPTIBILITY

THE MARXIST FOUNDATION

The social justice movement infiltrating American churches today didn't emerge from Christian theology or biblical scholarship. Its roots trace directly to the revolutionary philosophy of Karl Marx and the broader socialist movement of the 19th century. Understanding this genealogy is crucial for Christians who want to recognize why this ideology is fundamentally incompatible with biblical faith.

Marx's critique of capitalism was more theological than many realized. He viewed religion as "the opium of the people," a tool used by the ruling class to pacify the oppressed masses with promises of heavenly reward while they suffered earthly exploitation. In Marx's worldview, traditional Christianity was part of the problem, not the solution. It taught workers to accept their suffering rather than revolt against their oppressors.

The Marxist solution was revolutionary: overthrow the existing order through class struggle, redistribute wealth through collective ownership, and create a new society based on material equality rather than spiritual salvation. It was made as a replacement for religion with the intention to replace Christianity among the populace.

But Marx understood something that many Christians today have forgotten: people need meaning, purpose, and moral framework. Simply destroying religion wouldn't work unless you replaced it with something else. That replacement became what we now call social justice - a secular salvation narrative that promises redemption through political action rather than personal repentance.

The parallels are unmistakable. Traditional Christianity teaches that humans are fallen beings in need of divine salvation. Social justice teaches that humans are oppressed beings in need of political liberation. Christianity promises eternal life through faith in Christ. Social justice promises earthly paradise through revolutionary change. Christianity calls for individual repentance and transformation. Social justice demands collective guilt and systemic transformation.

The Catholic Response and Church Vulnerability

Ironically, the term "social justice" was first popularized not by Marx but by Catholic scholar Luigi Taparelli in the 1840s. Taparelli was responding to the same industrial inequalities that motivated Marx, but from a fundamentally different perspective. Where Marx saw class warfare as the solution, Taparelli emphasized human dignity, natural law, and the common good rooted in Christian anthropology.

The Catholic Church's development of social teaching, from Pope Leo XIII's "Rerum Novarum" in 1891 through subsequent papal encyclicals, represented a coherent Christian response to modern social problems. This teaching acknowledged troubles with economic inequality and worker exploitation while maintaining the primacy of spiritual salvation and individual moral responsibility.

Catholic social teaching succeeded in addressing social concerns without abandoning Christian orthodoxy because it was grounded in 2,000 years of theological development, natural law philosophy, and magisterial authority. The Church could speak authoritatively on social issues because it had a stable doctrinal foundation and institutional structure that prevented ideological capture.

Many churches lacked these safeguards. The principle of "sola scriptura" or "Scripture alone" had produced hundreds of denominations with competing interpretations of biblical teaching. Without a central teaching authority, churches were vulnerable to whatever intellectual currents happened to be popular in their surrounding culture.

More problematically, many denominations had already embraced theological liberalism by the early 20th century. Liberal theology, influenced by German higher criticism and evolutionary theory, had undermined confidence in biblical authority and supernatural Christianity. Churches that no longer believed in the literal truth of Scripture or the necessity of personal salvation were easy targets for secular ideologies that promised social transformation through human effort.

The Frankfurt School and Cultural Marxism

The direct transmission of Marxist ideas into American Christianity came through what became known as the Frankfurt School, a group of German intellectuals who fled Nazi Germany and established themselves at Columbia University in the 1930s. Figures like Herbert Marcuse, Theodor Adorno, and Max Horkheimer developed what they called "critical theory" - a sophisticated method for analyzing and undermining Western civilization from within.

Critical theory represented a crucial evolution in Marxist strategy. Classical Marxism had predicted that economic contradictions would lead to worker revolution in industrialized nations. When this failed to materialize, particularly in America, where capitalism had produced unprecedented prosperity for working classes, Marxist intellectuals needed a new approach.

The Frankfurt School's innovation was cultural rather than economic. Instead of focusing solely on class struggle, they expanded Marx's critique to include race, gender, sexuality, and other identity categories. Instead of waiting for economic collapse, they would undermine Western civilization by attacking its cultural foundations: Christianity, traditional family structures, patriotism, and objective truth itself.

This cultural Marxism proved far more effective than its economic predecessor. Where classical Marxism had failed to convince American workers that they were oppressed, cultural Marxism succeeded in convincing American Christians that they were oppressors. The strategy was brilliant in its simplicity: use Christian compassion and guilt as weapons against Christian civilization.

Herbert Marcuse's concept of "repressive tolerance" became particularly influential in religious circles. Marcuse argued that traditional tolerance - allowing different viewpoints to compete in the marketplace of ideas - actually perpetuated oppression by giving equal hearing to oppressive and liberating perspectives. True tolerance, he claimed, required suppressing oppressive viewpoints while promoting liberating ones.

This framework gave progressive Christians a theological justification for silencing conservative voices within their denominations. Traditional biblical teachings about sexuality, gender roles, and personal responsibility could be dismissed as "oppressive" and therefore unworthy of tolerance. Meanwhile, progressive interpretations that aligned with secular social justice goals were promoted as "liberating" and therefore morally superior.

Liberation Theology: Marxism in Christian Clothing

The most direct synthesis of Marxist ideology and Christian theology emerged in Latin America during the 1960s through liberation theology. Pioneered by figures like Gustavo Gutiérrez and Leonardo Boff, liberation theology explicitly merged Marx's class analysis with Christian salvation narratives.

Liberation theologians argued that God had a "preferential option for the poor" that required Christians to engage in political action against economic oppression. They reinterpreted biblical narratives through Marxist categories: the Exodus became a story of class struggle, Jesus became a revolutionary leader, and salvation became synonymous with political liberation.

This was explicit ideological fusion. Liberation theologians openly acknowledged their debt to Marx while claiming that his analysis was compatible with Christian faith. They argued that Marx's critique of capitalism revealed God's concern for the oppressed, making Marxist revolution a Christian duty.

The Catholic Church, under Pope John Paul II, firmly rejected liberation theology as incompatible with Christian orthodoxy. The Congregation for the Doctrine of the Faith, led by Cardinal Joseph Ratzinger (later Pope Benedict XVI), issued detailed critiques explaining why Marxist analysis contradicted fundamental Christian teachings about human nature, salvation, and the role of the Church.

But liberation theology found fertile ground in seminaries and denominations that lacked the Catholic or Orthodox Churches' doctrinal clarity and institutional resistance. Progressive theologians embraced liberation theology's methodology while adapting its focus from economic class to other identity categories: race, gender, sexuality, and immigration status.

The Philosophical Incompatibility

The fundamental problem with social justice ideology isn't its concern for the poor and oppressed. Christianity has always championed the vulnerable. The problem is its philosophical foundation, which contradicts core Christian teachings at every level.

Christianity teaches that humans are created in the image of God with inherent dignity and individual moral responsibility. Social justice ideology reduces humans to members of oppressor or oppressed groups, with moral worth determined by group identity rather than individual character or divine image.

Christianity teaches that sin is a universal human condition requiring divine grace for redemption. Social justice ideology teaches that sin is primarily systemic and can be eliminated through political action and social restructuring.

Christianity also teaches that ultimate justice belongs to God and will be fully realized in the eschaton. Social justice ideology demands immediate earthly justice achieved through human effort and revolutionary change.

Christianity teaches forgiveness, reconciliation, and love for enemies. Social justice ideology promotes perpetual grievance, group conflict, and moral condemnation of oppressor classes.

These aren't minor theological differences that can be resolved through dialogue or compromise. They represent incompatible worldviews with different anthropologies, different soteriologies, and different eschatologies. A church cannot embrace both without abandoning one or the other.

The tragedy is that many well-meaning Christians have been deceived into thinking they can synthesize these worldviews. They've been told that social justice represents the "prophetic tradition" of Christianity, that concern for the oppressed requires adoption of Marxist analysis, and that opposition to social justice ideology reveals lack of Christian compassion.

This deception has been remarkably successful because it exploits the genuine Christian virtues of compassion, humility, and concern for justice, while redirecting them toward anti-Christian ends. Christians who would never knowingly embrace Marxist ideology have been gradually conditioned to accept its premises when presented in religious language.

The result is churches filled with people who think they're following Christ while actually following Marx, who believe they're promoting biblical justice while actually undermining biblical authority, and who imagine they're serving God while actually serving an ideology that seeks to replace God with political revolution.

Biblical Misinterpretation and Christian Susceptibility

The success of social justice ideology in infiltrating American churches isn't merely due to external pressure or clever marketing. Christians have proven uniquely susceptible to this deception because they consistently misinterpret key biblical passages, creating theological vulnerabilities that social justice advocates expertly exploit.

Two verses in particular have become weapons in the hands of those seeking to transform Christianity into a vehicle for Marxist ideology: Galatians 3:28 and Matthew 7:1. These passages, ripped from their proper context and twisted beyond recognition, have provided the theological foundation for abandoning biblical discernment and embracing secular social justice narratives.

The Galatians 3:28 Deception

"There is neither Jew nor Gentile, neither slave nor free, nor is there male and female, for you are all one in Christ Jesus" (Galatians

3:28). Social justice advocates have weaponized this verse to argue that Christianity recognizes no meaningful distinctions between people groups, cultures, or even biological realities. They claim it supports their vision of a colorblind, genderless society where all differences are erased in the name of equality.

This interpretation reveals either profound biblical illiteracy or deliberate deception. Paul's statement in Galatians 3:28 addresses spiritual equality before God in matters of salvation, not the elimination of all earthly distinctions or cultural differences. The context makes this abundantly clear - Paul is explaining that both Jews and Gentiles can receive salvation through faith in Christ, not that Jews and Gentiles are identical in all respects.

The verse speaks to God's willingness to accept anyone into salvation who meets the requirements and genuinely repents. It does not mean there are no literal divisions on earth or that people are not different from one another. People are different. Cultures are different. Some cultures are not compatible with others. There is nothing wrong with noticing or acknowledging these realities.

If Galatians 3:28 truly meant the elimination of all distinctions, it would contradict the rest of Scripture. Paul himself, in the same letter, acknowledges cultural and ethnic differences throughout his ministry. In 1 Corinthians 7:17-24, he explicitly tells people to remain in the condition they were in when called, including slaves remaining slaves if they cannot gain freedom. In Ephesians 5:22-33, he outlines distinct roles for husbands and wives. In 1 Timothy 2:12, he establishes different roles for men and women in church leadership.

The social justice interpretation of Galatians 3:28 would make Paul contradict himself repeatedly throughout his epistles. More seriously, it would contradict Christ himself, who clearly recognized ethnic and cultural distinctions in his earthly ministry. When the Canaanite woman approached Jesus seeking healing for her daughter, he initially refused, saying, "I was sent only to the lost sheep of Israel" and "It is not right to take the children's bread and toss it to the dogs" (Matthew 15:24-26).

Christ's response wasn't sinful racism, as he is incapable of sin. By contrast, he recognized his primary mission to the Jewish people and acknowledgment of legitimate ethnic and cultural boundaries. Since Christ cannot sin by his nature, maintaining community solidarity with one's ethnic group and making judgments based on cultural differences cannot be inherently sinful.

The "Judge Not" Heresy

Perhaps no biblical passage has been more thoroughly corrupted than Matthew 7:1: "Do not judge, or you too will be judged." Social justice advocates have transformed this verse into a universal prohibition against moral discernment, theological evaluation, or cultural criticism. Any attempt to identify sin, false teaching, or destructive behavior is dismissed with the simple phrase "judge not."

This interpretation has created a generation of Christians who are spiritually defenseless against error and evil. They've been conditioned to believe that making moral judgments is itself immoral, that identifying false teaching is unloving, and that calling sin "sin" violates Christ's command.

But Christ's teaching in Matthew 7:1-5 is about hypocrisy, not about abandoning all moral discernment. The full passage reads: "Do not judge, or you too will be judged. For in the same way you judge others, you will be judged, and with the measure you use, it will be measured to you. Why do you look at the speck of sawdust in your brother's eye and pay no attention to the plank in your own eye? How can you say to your brother, 'Let me take the speck out of your eye,' when all the time there is a plank in your own eye? You hypocrite, first take the plank out of your own eye, and then you will see clearly to remove the speck from your brother's eye."

The passage concludes with Christ instructing his followers to remove the speck from their brother's eye - after first addressing their own sin. This is a call to righteous judgment, not the abandonment of judgment altogether. Christ is warning against hypocritical judgment while commanding proper judgment based on biblical standards.

The rest of Scripture makes this interpretation unmistakable. In John 7:24, Christ explicitly commands, "Stop judging by mere appearances, but instead judge correctly." In 1 Corinthians 5:12-13, Paul asks, "What business is it of mine to judge those outside the church? Are you not to judge those inside? God will judge those outside. 'Expel the wicked person from among you.'" In 1 Thessalonians 5:21-22, believers are commanded to "test everything" and "reject whatever is harmful."

The biblical model requires Christians to make careful moral and theological judgments based on Scripture. They must identify false teachers (Matthew 7:15-20), confront sin within the church (Matthew 18:15-17), and test all teaching against the Word of God (Acts 17:11). The "judge not" interpretation makes all of this impossible.

The Devastating Results

The misinterpretation of these key passages has created the perfect storm for social justice infiltration. Churches that cannot make theological judgments cannot identify false teaching. Christians who believe all distinctions are meaningless cannot defend biblical truth about gender, sexuality, or cultural differences. Believers who think moral discernment is unloving cannot confront sin or call for repentance.

This theological disarmament has led directly to the problems we identified in Chapter 1. Churches avoid discussing sin because that would require "judging" behavior. Pastors refuse to address controversial biblical teachings because that might seem "divisive." Congregations accept false doctrine because questioning it would violate the "judge not" principle.

The lack of biblical discernment has created a shallow understanding of Christianity that focuses on feelings rather than truth, therapy rather than transformation, and social activism rather than spiritual salvation. When churches cannot distinguish between biblical justice and social justice, between Christian love and secular tolerance, between Gospel truth and cultural trends, they inevitably drift toward whatever ideology happens to be popular in their surrounding culture.

Conclusion: The Perfect Deception

Social justice ideology in many ways became the perfect deception for American Christians because it exploits their genuine virtues

29

while undermining their theological foundation. It appeals to Christian compassion while promoting anti-Christian anthropology. It uses Christian vocabulary while advancing secular goals. It promises to fulfill Christian ideals while destroying Christian faith.

The historical progression is clear: Marxist intellectuals developed cultural criticism as a more effective strategy than economic revolution. Liberation theologians provided the theological framework for merging Marxist analysis with Christian language. Progressive seminaries and denominations embraced this synthesis while abandoning biblical authority. Local churches, lacking theological discernment and biblical literacy, proved unable to resist the infiltration.

The misinterpretation of key biblical passages provided the final piece of the puzzle. Christians who could no longer make theological judgments or acknowledge meaningful distinctions between people groups became sitting ducks for ideologies that promised to solve social problems through political action rather than spiritual transformation.

The result is churches filled with people who think they're following Christ while actually following Marx, who believe they're promoting biblical justice while actually undermining biblical authority, and who imagine they're serving the oppressed while actually serving an ideology that seeks to replace Christianity with revolutionary politics.

This is the logical result of abandoning biblical authority, embracing theological liberalism, and prioritizing cultural acceptance over Gospel truth. American churches have proven uniquely vulnerable to this deception because they lack the doctrinal stability, institutional authority, and theological depth necessary to resist sophisticated ideological infiltration.

The tragedy occurs when churches become active participants in their own deception, using Christian resources and Christian platforms to advance anti-Christian goals. They've become the Trojan horse through which secular ideology conquers Christian civilization from within.

But recognition is the first step toward resistance. Christians who understand the true origins and nature of social justice ideology can begin to rebuild the theological defenses that previous generations allowed to crumble. The question is whether enough believers will choose biblical truth over cultural acceptance before the deception becomes complete.

3

THE SIX WARNING SIGNS - IDENTIFYING COMPROMISED CHURCHES

THE CANCER OF SOCIAL JUSTICE IDEOLOGY DOESN'T ANNOUNCE ITSELF with obvious symptoms. Churches don't suddenly replace their crosses with hammer-and-sickle symbols or begin their services with readings from Marx's "Das Kapital." The infiltration is subtle, gradual, and often disguised as spiritual progress or cultural relevance.

But the signs are there for those who know what to look for. After years of observing this corruption spread through American churches, I've identified six clear warning signs that indicate a congregation has been compromised by social justice ideology. These mark full departures from biblical Christianity that signal a church's abandonment of its divine mission.

If your church exhibits even one of these signs, you should be concerned. If it exhibits multiple signs, you should leave immediately. The spiritual health of your family depends on recognizing these warning signs before the damage becomes irreversible.

Sign 1: Women Pastors

The first and most obvious sign of a compromised church is the presence of women in pastoral leadership roles. Before someone gets too outraged on this topic, no one is commenting on women's capabilities, intelligence, or spiritual maturity, but instead biblical obedience and God's design for church governance.

The Apostle Paul's instruction in 1 Timothy 2:12 is unambiguous: "But I do not allow a woman to teach or exercise authority over a man, but to remain quiet." The context makes clear that Paul is addressing church leadership and the teaching of doctrine to mixed congregations.

Paul explains his reasoning in the following verses: "For Adam was formed first, then Eve. And Adam was not the one deceived; it was the woman who was deceived and became a sinner" (1 Timothy 2:13-14). The prohibition against women in pastoral authority isn't based on temporary cultural conditions but on the permanent realities of creation and the fall. God established a specific order for church leadership that reflects his design for human relationships and spiritual authority.

This teaching is reinforced throughout Scripture. In 1 Corinthians 14:34-35, Paul writes, "Women should remain silent in the churches. They are not allowed to speak, but must be in submission, as the law says. If they want to inquire about something, they should ask their own husbands at home; for it is disgraceful for a woman to speak in the church." In Titus 1:6-9, Paul outlines the qualifications for elders, consistently using masculine pronouns and referring to the elder as "the husband of one wife."

Churches that ordain women pastors have made a deliberate decision to reject biblical authority in favor of cultural pressure. They've decided that modern feminist ideology trumps apostolic teaching, that contemporary sensibilities matter more than divine command, and that cultural acceptance is more important than biblical obedience.

The justifications offered for women's ordination reveal the depth of this rebellion against Scripture. Progressive churches claim that Paul's instructions were "just for the culture at the time," but the Bible never indicates that any of its moral or ecclesiastical teachings are temporary cultural accommodations. If Christians can dismiss Paul's teaching about women in leadership as culturally outdated, they can dismiss any biblical teaching that conflicts with modern sensibilities.

Others argue that Paul was addressing specific problems in Ephesus or Corinth, not establishing universal principles for church governance. But Paul's reasoning from creation and the fall demonstrates that he's establishing permanent principles based on God's design for human relationships, not addressing temporary local issues.

The most sophisticated argument claims that Paul's prohibition applies only to wives teaching their husbands, not to women teaching men generally. This interpretation requires tortured exegesis that ignores the clear context of church leadership and the consistent pattern of masculine leadership throughout Scripture.

God's Design for Church Leadership

The prohibition against women pastors reflects God's wisdom in establishing clear authority structures that promote order, unity, and spiritual health within the church. God designed men and women with complementary roles that reflect different aspects of his character and serve different functions in his kingdom.

Men are called to spiritual leadership not because they're superior to women but because God has equipped them for the specific responsibilities of pastoral authority: doctrinal teaching, church discipline, and spiritual protection of the congregation. This leadership role requires the willingness to make difficult decisions, confront sin directly, and maintain doctrinal boundaries even when it's unpopular.

Women are called to equally important but different roles that utilize their unique gifts and perspectives. Titus 2:3-5 describes older women teaching younger women about marriage, motherhood, and godly living. Priscilla worked alongside her husband Aquila to instruct Apollos in the way of God more accurately (Acts 18:26). Women served as deaconesses, prophetesses, and vital contributors to church life without violating the principle of male pastoral authority.

Churches with women pastors inevitably experience the consequences of rejecting God's design. Without clear authority structures, these congregations often struggle with doctrinal confusion, leadership conflicts, and spiritual instability. The nurturing, consensus-building approach that characterizes feminine leadership - valuable in its proper sphere - proves inadequate for the demanding responsibilities of pastoral authority.

More fundamentally, churches that ordain women pastors have demonstrated their willingness to prioritize cultural acceptance over biblical obedience. If they'll reject clear apostolic teaching on church leadership, they'll reject any biblical teaching that conflicts with contemporary values. The ordination of women pastors is rarely an isolated compromise - it's typically the first step in a broader abandonment of biblical authority.

Sign 2: Cherry-Picking Feel-Good Bible Passages

The second warning sign of a compromised church is the consistent pattern of preaching only from "attractive" biblical passages while avoiding the difficult, challenging, or controversial parts of Scripture. These churches have embraced what pastor Tim Keller calls "the attractive gospel," a sanitized version of Christianity that emphasizes God's love while ignoring his wrath, promises blessing while avoiding the cost of discipleship, and offers comfort while demanding no real change.

Walk into most American churches on any given Sunday, and you'll hear sermons from the same predictable passages: John 3:16 about God's love, Jeremiah 29:11 about God's plans for prosperity, Romans 8:28 about all things working together for good, and Philippians 4:13 about doing all things through Christ who strengthens. These verses are preached repeatedly, often out of context, while vast portions of Scripture remain unexplored.

What you won't hear are sermons about God's wrath against sin, the reality of hell, the narrow gate that leads to life, or the cost of following Christ. Pastors avoid passages about church discipline, sexual morality, financial stewardship, or the persecution that awaits faithful Christians. They skip over the imprecatory psalms, the warnings in Hebrews, the judgments in Revelation, and Christ's harsh words to the Pharisees.

This selective approach to Scripture reveals a rejection of the

Gospel itself. The core of Christianity is the good news that God has provided salvation for sinners who deserve judgment. The Gospel only makes sense in light of human sinfulness, divine holiness, and the reality of eternal punishment for those who reject Christ.

Churches that preach only the "attractive gospel" rob their congregations of the full counsel of God. They produce believers who know nothing about the cost of discipleship, the reality of spiritual warfare, or the necessity of holiness. These Christians are spiritually malnourished, lacking the theological foundation necessary to withstand trials, resist temptation, or discern false teaching.

The Biblical Model of Comprehensive Teaching

The Apostle Paul provides the model for faithful biblical preaching in his farewell address to the Ephesian elders: "For I have not hesitated to proclaim to you the whole will of God" (Acts 20:27). Paul didn't limit his teaching to comfortable topics or popular themes, but proclaimed the entire counsel of God, including the difficult truths that his audience might not want to hear.

Paul's ministry included warnings about false teachers, instructions about church discipline, teachings on sexual morality, and exhortations about the cost of following Christ. He didn't avoid controversial topics or soften difficult truths to maintain popularity. His goal wasn't to make people feel good about themselves but instead to make them holy through the transforming power of God's Word.

Christ himself modeled this comprehensive approach to teaching. His sermons included both comfort and challenge, both promises and warnings, both grace and judgment. He spoke about God's love and God's wrath, about salvation and damnation, about the narrow gate and the broad road. Many of his teachings were so challenging that large crowds stopped following him (John 6:66).

The writer of Hebrews explains why comprehensive biblical teaching is essential: "For the word of God is alive and active. Sharper than any double-edged sword, it penetrates even to dividing soul and spirit, joints and marrow; it judges the thoughts and attitudes of the heart" (Hebrews 4:12). God's Word is designed to convict, challenge, and transform.

Churches that avoid difficult biblical passages are performing spiritual malpractice. They're like doctors who refuse to diagnose serious illnesses because the news might upset their patients. The result is congregations filled with people who think they're spiritually healthy when they're actually dying from unaddressed sin and theological ignorance.

The Prosperity Gospel Connection

The cherry-picking of feel-good passages often connects directly to prosperity gospel theology, which promises health, wealth, and happiness to faithful believers. Prosperity preachers love verses like Jeremiah 29:11 ("'For I know the plans I have for you,' declares the Lord, 'plans to prosper you and not to harm you, to give you hope and a future'") while ignoring the context - God's promise to the Jewish exiles that they would return to their homeland after 70 years of captivity.

They quote Philippians 4:13 ("I can do all this through him who gives me strength") as a promise of unlimited success while ignoring the context. Paul's contentment included both abundance and need, including imprisonment and suffering for the Gospel. They emphasize 3 John 2 ("I pray that you may enjoy good health and that all may go well with you") while ignoring the thousands of verses about suffering, persecution, and the cost of discipleship.

This selective use of Scripture produces a false gospel that promises earthly blessing without heavenly transformation, material prosperity without spiritual maturity, and temporal comfort without eternal significance. It attracts crowds by telling people what they want to hear while failing to deliver what they actually need - conviction of sin, call to repentance, and transformation through the power of the Gospel.

Christ warned against this approach in Matthew 7:13-14: "Enter through the narrow gate. For wide is the gate and broad is the road that leads to destruction, and many enter through it. But small is the gate and narrow the road that leads to life, and only a few find it." The attractive gospel makes the gate wide and the road broad by removing the demands of discipleship and the reality of spiritual warfare.

Sign 3: Corporate Slogans Replacing Mission Statements

The third warning sign of a compromised church is the replacement of detailed, biblically-grounded mission statements with meaningless corporate slogans designed for marketing rather than ministry. When churches begin operating like businesses competing for market share, they adopt the language and methods of secular corporations, treating congregants like consumers and the Gospel like a product to be sold.

Traditional churches understood their mission in theological terms rooted in Scripture and refined through centuries of Christian thought. Their statements of belief were comprehensive, demanding, and substantive - documents that required careful study and serious commitment. These statements didn't just describe what the church believed; they explained why those beliefs mattered and how they should shape Christian living.

Consider this example of a classical statement of belief from a faithful church: "We believe that Jesus Christ is the eternal Son of God, who through His perfect life and sacrificial death atoned for the sins of all who will trust in Him, alone, for salvation. We believe that God is gracious and faithful to His people not simply as individuals but as families in successive generations according to His Covenant promises. We believe that the Holy Spirit indwells God's people and gives them the strength and wisdom to trust Christ and follow Him. We believe that Jesus will return, bodily and visibly, to judge all mankind and to receive His people to Himself. We believe that all aspects of our lives are to be lived to the glory of God under the Lordship of Jesus Christ."

This statement is long, detailed, and theologically rich. It requires thought to understand and commitment to embrace. It addresses fundamental Christian doctrines: the nature of Christ, the means of salvation, the work of the Holy Spirit, the second coming, and the comprehensive lordship of Christ over all of life. Someone reading this statement knows exactly what this church believes and what will be expected of members.

Compare that substantial theological foundation to the vapid slogans that have replaced mission statements in compromised churches: "Listen. Learn. Love." "Connect. Grow. Serve." "Believe. Belong. Become." "Real People. Real Faith. Real Life." These phrases sound appealing and feel good, but they're utterly meaningless. They could apply to any organization, any philosophy, or any self-help program.

The Consumer Church Mentality

The adoption of corporate slogans reveals a fundamental shift in how churches understand their purpose and their relationship with their congregations. Instead of seeing themselves as shepherds responsible for the spiritual welfare of their flocks, pastors begin thinking like CEOs responsible for customer satisfaction and market growth.

This consumer mentality transforms every aspect of church life. Worship services become entertainment productions designed to attract and retain audiences. Sermons become motivational speeches crafted to inspire rather than convict. Church programs become amenities offered to meet consumer preferences. Even the Gospel itself becomes a product marketed to meet felt needs rather than actual spiritual requirements.

The language of consumer Christianity pervades these churches. They talk about "church shopping," "meeting people where they are," "relevant messages," and "user-friendly services." They conduct focus groups to determine what people want to hear, demographic studies to identify target markets, and satisfaction surveys to measure success.

This approach produces churches that look successful by worldly standards including large attendance, impressive facilities, substantial budgets, and positive community reputation, while failing completely in their spiritual mission. They attract consumers looking for religious entertainment but repel seekers looking for authentic spiritual transformation.

God's Design for Church Identity

Scripture presents a radically different vision of church identity and mission. The church was never intended to be a business competing for customers but the body of Christ called to proclaim the Gospel and make disciples. Its success isn't measured by attendance numbers or budget growth but by faithfulness to God's Word and the spiritual maturity of its members.

The Great Commission provides the church's fundamental mission: "Therefore go and make disciples of all nations, baptizing them in the name of the Father and of the Son and of the Holy Spirit, and teaching them to obey everything I have commanded you" (Matthew 28:19-20). This mission is specific, demanding, and measurable - make disciples who are baptized and taught to obey Christ's commands.

Paul describes the church's purpose in Ephesians 4:11-16: "So Christ himself gave the apostles, the prophets, the evangelists, the pastors and teachers, to equip his people for works of service, so that the body of Christ may be built up until we all reach unity in the faith and in the knowledge of the Son of God and become mature, attaining to the whole measure of the fullness of Christ. Then we will no longer be infants, tossed back and forth by the waves, and blown here and there by every wind of teaching and by the cunning and craftiness of people in their deceitful scheming. Instead, speaking the truth in love, we will grow to become in every respect the mature body of him who is the head, that is, Christ."

This passage reveals God's design for church ministry: equipping believers for service, building up the body of Christ, promoting unity in faith and knowledge, developing spiritual maturity, and protecting against false teaching. None of these goals can be achieved through corporate slogans or consumer marketing strategies.

Churches that replace substantial theological statements with marketing slogans have abandoned their divine mission in favor of worldly success metrics. They've chosen to be popular rather than prophetic, relevant rather than righteous, and attractive rather than authentic. The result is institutions that may look like churches but function like businesses, attracting crowds while failing to transform lives.

These churches actively undermine it by teaching people to approach Christianity as consumers rather than disciples. They produce believers who evaluate churches based on personal preferences rather than biblical faithfulness, who seek spiritual entertainment rather than spiritual transformation, and who view the Gospel as a product to be consumed rather than a truth to be obeyed.

When churches abandon their theological identity for corporate branding, they lose their reason for existence. They may attract crowds, generate revenue, and receive positive publicity, but they're no longer churches in any biblical sense. They've become religious businesses using Christian vocabulary to sell secular products to spiritual consumers.

Sign 4: Race and Racism Focus

The fourth warning sign of a compromised church is an obsessive focus on race and racism that replaces the Gospel's message of unity in Christ with the world's message of perpetual division and grievance. These churches have abandoned the biblical teaching that believers are "all one in Christ Jesus" (Galatians 3:28) in favor of secular ideologies that demand Christians see themselves primarily through racial categories rather than their identity as children of God.

Churches exhibiting this warning sign regularly preach about "white privilege," "systemic racism," and "racial reconciliation" while avoiding the Gospel's actual message about reconciliation between God and man. They promote books like "White Fragility" from the pulpit, organize "racial justice" workshops, and encourage white congregants to confess sins they never committed based solely on their skin color.

This racial obsession represents a fundamental departure from biblical Christianity. Scripture teaches that God "made from one man every nation of mankind to live on all the face of the earth" (Acts 17:26) and that in Christ "there is neither Jew nor Gentile" (Galatians 3:28). The Gospel breaks down racial barriers by creating a new identity that transcends ethnic distinctions - the family of God united by faith in Jesus Christ.

But social justice ideology demands the opposite. It insists that racial identity is permanent, that racial differences are the most important aspect of human relationships, and that racial grievances must be constantly rehearsed rather than forgiven and forgotten. This ideology turns the Gospel's message of reconciliation into a weapon of division, using Christian guilt and compassion to advance secular political goals.

The biblical response to racial division isn't endless focus on racial differences but the proclamation of spiritual unity in Christ. When the early church faced ethnic tensions between Jewish and Gentile believers, the apostles didn't organize racial reconciliation workshops or demand that Jews confess their ethnic privilege. They preached the Gospel message that both groups were equally sinful, equally loved by God, and equally saved by grace through faith in Christ.

Christ's Example of Proper Ethnic Recognition

The most devastating refutation of the racial obsession comes from Christ himself. When the Canaanite woman approached Jesus seeking healing for her daughter, he initially refused her request, saying, "I was sent only to the lost sheep of Israel" (Matthew 15:24). When she persisted, he responded, "It is not right to take the children's bread and toss it to the dogs" (Matthew 15:26).

Modern racial justice advocates would condemn Christ's response as racist, but Scripture presents it as an example of proper ethnic recognition and mission priorities. Christ acknowledged legitimate ethnic and cultural boundaries while maintaining his primary mission to the Jewish people. He wasn't expressing racial hatred but demonstrating that ethnic distinctions are real and that different groups have different roles in God's redemptive plan.

Since Christ cannot sin by his nature, his recognition of ethnic differences and his prioritization of his own people cannot be inherently sinful. This means that maintaining community solidarity with one's ethnic group and making judgments based on cultural differences are not violations of Christian love but expressions of the wisdom and order that God built into human society.

Churches that condemn all ethnic awareness as sinful racism are actually condemning Christ himself. They've adopted a secular ideology that demands the elimination of all ethnic distinctions in favor of a colorblind society that exists nowhere in Scripture and nowhere in human history.

The Destruction of Biblical Unity

The racial obsession destroys the very unity it claims to promote. Instead of bringing believers together around their common identity in Christ, it divides them into oppressor and oppressed categories based on skin color. White Christians are taught to feel perpetual guilt for sins they never committed, while minority Christians are encouraged to nurse grievances against their white brothers and sisters in Christ.

This division is antithetical to the Gospel's message of reconciliation. Paul writes in 2 Corinthians 5:17-20: "Therefore, if anyone is in Christ, the new creation has come: The old has gone, the new is here! All this is from God, who reconciled us to himself through Christ and gave us the ministry of reconciliation: that God was reconciling the world to himself in Christ, not counting people's sins against them. And he has committed to us the message of reconciliation. We are therefore Christ's ambassadors, as though God were making his appeal through us."

The ministry of reconciliation focuses on bringing people to God through Christ, not on perpetuating racial grievances or demanding reparations for historical injustices. Churches that prioritize racial reconciliation over Gospel reconciliation have abandoned their biblical mission in favor of secular social work.

Moreover, the racial obsession typically serves as a gateway to other social justice causes. Churches that begin by focusing on racial issues inevitably expand to include gender ideology, sexual revolution, and economic redistribution. The underlying worldview that society is divided into oppressor and oppressed groups requiring political liberation applies to every category that secular leftists want to weaponize.

Sign 5: Leadership Avoiding Scriptural Discussion

The fifth warning sign of a compromised church is pastoral leadership that refuses to engage in serious scriptural discussion with congregants, particularly when those discussions might challenge the church's direction or expose theological problems. These pastors view themselves as CEOs rather than shepherds, treating their congregations like customers rather than sheep entrusted to their spiritual care.

Biblical church leadership operates on the principle of elder accountability and congregational involvement in doctrinal matters. The early church model shows believers examining Scripture together, testing all teaching against God's Word, and holding their leaders accountable to biblical standards. The Bereans were commended for examining the Scriptures daily to verify Paul's teaching (Acts 17:11), and Paul himself submitted his ministry to the scrutiny of other apostles and church leaders.

But compromised churches operate more like corporations than biblical communities. The pastor functions as an untouchable executive who makes unilateral decisions about church direction, doctrine, and practice. Congregants who raise biblical concerns are dismissed, redirected to subordinates, or told that such discussions are inappropriate for laypeople.

This authoritarian approach reveals a fundamental insecurity about the church's theological foundation. Pastors who are confident in their biblical positions welcome scriptural discussion because they know their teaching can withstand scrutiny. Leaders who avoid such discussions typically do so because they know their positions cannot be defended from Scripture.

The Biblical Model of Pastoral Accountability

Scripture presents a radically different model of church leadership based on accountability, transparency, and shared commitment to God's Word. Pastors are called to be shepherds who feed the flock with knowledge and understanding (Jeremiah 3:15), not CEOs who make executive decisions without consultation or explanation.

The qualifications for church elders in 1 Timothy 3:1-7 and Titus 1:5-9 emphasize character, biblical knowledge, and teaching ability. These men must be "able to teach" and "able to give instruction in sound doctrine and also to rebuke those who contradict it" (Titus 1:9). The emphasis on teaching ability assumes that elders will engage in substantive biblical discussion with their congregations.

Paul's instructions to Timothy reveal the proper relationship between pastoral authority and congregational involvement: "All Scripture is God-breathed and is useful for teaching, rebuking, correcting and training in righteousness, so that the servant of God may be thoroughly equipped for every good work" (2 Timothy 3:16-17). The pastor's authority comes from Scripture, not from his position, and his teaching must be evaluated against biblical standards.

The early church practiced this model of shared scriptural engagement. When disputes arose about circumcision and Gentile inclusion, the apostles and elders came together to examine the issue biblically (Acts 15:1-35). When Paul confronted Peter about his hypocrisy regarding Gentile fellowship, he did so publicly and based his argument on Gospel principles (Galatians 2:11-14).

Churches that follow the biblical model encourage congregational involvement in doctrinal discussions, welcome questions about church direction, and provide biblical justification for their decisions. They understand that pastoral authority serves the Word of God rather than replacing it.

The Consequences of Pastoral Authoritarianism

Churches where pastors avoid scriptural discussion inevitably drift from biblical truth because they lack the accountability mechanisms that God designed to keep church leadership faithful to his Word. Without congregational oversight and biblical scrutiny, pastors become susceptible to cultural pressure, personal ambition, and theological error.

This drift typically follows a predictable pattern. First, the pastor begins making decisions based on pragmatic considerations rather than biblical principles. Church programs, worship styles, and even doctrinal positions are evaluated based on their effectiveness in attracting crowds or generating revenue rather than their faithfulness to Scripture.

Second, the pastor surrounds himself with staff members and board members who share his vision rather than his commitment to biblical truth. These supporters function more like corporate yes-men than biblical elders, affirming the pastor's decisions rather than holding him accountable to God's Word.

Third, congregants who raise biblical concerns are marginalized, silenced, or driven away. The church develops a culture where questioning leadership is viewed as disloyalty rather than spiritual responsibility. This creates an echo chamber where false teaching can flourish without challenge.

Finally, the church abandons biblical Christianity entirely while maintaining Christian vocabulary and religious rituals. The congregation continues to sing Christian songs, pray Christian prayers, and use Christian language, but the substance of their faith has been replaced by secular ideology dressed in religious clothing.

Sign 6: Online Growth Over Local Community

The sixth and final warning sign of a compromised church is the prioritization of online growth and digital engagement over local community and physical fellowship. These churches have embraced the lie that virtual connection can replace the embodied relationships that God designed for his people, treating the church like a media company rather than the body of Christ.

The COVID-19 pandemic accelerated this trend as churches were forced to move their services online. But what began as a temporary accommodation has become a permanent feature of many churches that discovered they could reach larger audiences and generate more revenue through digital platforms than through traditional in-person ministry.

Churches exhibiting this warning sign measure success by online metrics of views, likes, shares, and subscribers, rather than spiritual fruit in the lives of their members. They invest more resources in video production, social media marketing, and digital content creation than in pastoral care, discipleship, and local community building.

This digital-first approach fundamentally misunderstands the nature of the church and the requirements of Christian fellowship. The church isn't a content delivery system or an entertainment platform - it's the body of Christ, a living organism that requires physical presence and embodied relationships to function properly.

The Biblical Necessity of Physical Fellowship

Scripture consistently emphasizes the importance of physical presence and embodied relationships within the Christian community. The church is described as a body (1 Corinthians 12:12-27), a building (Ephesians 2:19-22), and a family (1 Timothy 3:15) - all metaphors that require physical proximity and tangible interaction.

Paul's description of the church as Christ's body makes this particularly clear: "Just as a body, though one, has many parts, but all its many parts form one body, so it is with Christ. For we were all baptized by one Spirit so as to form one body—whether Jews or Gentiles, slave or free—and we were all given the one Spirit to drink. Even so the body is not made up of one part but of many" (1 Corinthians 12:12-14).

The body metaphor breaks down completely in a digital environment. Body parts cannot function properly when separated from the whole, and virtual connection cannot provide the mutual support, accountability, and care that physical fellowship enables. Romans 12:4-5 reinforces this truth: "For just as each of us has one body with many members, and these members do not all have the same function, so in Christ we, though many, form one body, and each member belongs to all the others."

The writer of Hebrews provides the most direct command regarding physical fellowship: "And let us consider how we may spur one another on toward love and good deeds, not giving up meeting together, as some are in the habit of doing, but encouraging one another—and all the more as you see the Day approaching" (Hebrews 10:24-25).

This passage makes clear that physical gathering isn't optional for Christians - it's a biblical command that becomes more important as Christ's return approaches. The encouragement, accountability, and mutual support described in this passage cannot be replicated through digital platforms.

The Spiritual Warfare of Isolation

The prioritization of online ministry over physical fellowship plays directly into Satan's strategy of isolation and division. The devil's goal is to separate believers from one another and from the strengthening influence of corporate worship and mutual accountability. Digital church attendance makes this separation easier by allowing people to consume religious content without submitting to the spiritual disciplines of embodied community.

Online church attendance enables a consumer mentality that treats worship like entertainment and the church like a service provider. People can watch sermons in their pajamas, skip parts they don't like, and avoid the uncomfortable aspects of Christian fellowship of accountability, service, and sacrificial love for difficult people.

This isolation is spiritually devastating. Christians who lack physical fellowship become vulnerable to false teaching, moral compromise, and spiritual discouragement. They miss the iron-sharpening-iron relationships (Proverbs 27:17) that God designed to promote spiritual growth and maturity.

The COVID-19 lockdowns provided a perfect example of this spiritual warfare. Churches that prioritized online ministry during the pandemic often discovered that many of their members never returned to in-person worship. These people had become accustomed to the convenience and comfort of digital consumption and lost their commitment to the demanding but necessary work of embodied Christian community.

The Sacramental Impossibility

Perhaps the most obvious problem with online church is the impossibility of properly administering the sacraments in a digital environment. Baptism and communion, the two sacraments that virtually all Christian traditions recognize, require physical presence and cannot be meaningfully performed through video screens.

Some churches have attempted to solve this problem by encouraging people to baptize themselves or take communion with crackers and grape juice at home while watching online services. These innovations reveal a fundamental misunderstanding of sacramental theology and the communal nature of Christian worship.

Baptism represents death to self and resurrection in Christ, administered by church leadership as a public declaration of faith and incorporation into the Christian community. Self-baptism eliminates the communal aspect and reduces the sacrament to a private ritual without ecclesiastical authority or community witness.

Communion is the believer's participation in Christ's body and blood, shared with the Christian community as an expression of unity and mutual commitment. Home communion eliminates the communal aspect and reduces the sacrament to individual consumption of religious symbols.

Churches that prioritize online ministry over sacramental worship have essentially abandoned two of the most important practices that Christ commanded his followers to observe. They've chosen digital convenience over divine command, virtual connection over sacramental grace.

Conclusion: The Pattern of Compromise

These six warning signs rarely appear in isolation. Churches that exhibit one sign typically develop others as the underlying compromise with biblical authority spreads throughout the congregation. The pattern is predictable: theological liberalism leads to cultural accommodation, which leads to mission drift, which leads to spiritual death.

The progression often begins with seemingly minor compromises of bringing in contemporary music, casual dress, or seeker-friendly services. But these surface changes reflect deeper theological shifts that eventually manifest in the six warning signs we've identified. Churches that prioritize cultural relevance over biblical faithfulness inevitably abandon both.

These churches produce believers who evaluate churches based on personal preferences rather than biblical faithfulness, who seek spiritual entertainment rather than spiritual transformation, and who view the Gospel as a product to be consumed rather than a truth to be obeyed.

But recognition of these warning signs provides hope for faithful Christians who want to find or build authentic Christian communities. Churches that avoid these compromises still exist and can be found by those willing to seek them out.

4

THE PROSPERITY GOSPEL
HERESY - WHEN GREED
MASQUERADES AS GOSPEL

THE MOST FINANCIALLY SUCCESSFUL PREACHERS IN AMERICA TODAY ARE selling a counterfeit that promises everything Christ never offered while avoiding everything he actually taught. This false gospel has infected American Christianity like a cancer, transforming churches into profit centers and believers into customers in a spiritual market-place that would make the money changers in the temple blush with shame.

The prosperity gospel, also known as the "health and wealth" gospel or "name it and claim it" theology, teaches that God wants all believers to be healthy, wealthy, and successful in this life. According to this heresy, faith is a force that can be used to manipulate God into providing material blessings, sickness is always a sign of insufficient faith, and poverty indicates spiritual failure. It directly contradicts Psalm 116:15, "Precious in the sight of the Lord is the death of his faithful saints," implying that God rewards suffering and martyrdom, not a comfortable life.

The prosperity gospel is a perversion of Christianity that replaces the true Gospel with a lie so seductive and so destructive that it damns souls while enriching the false teachers who promote it. It represents the complete inversion of Christ's teaching, turning the narrow gate into a wide highway paved with fool's gold.

The damage extends far beyond the obvious financial exploitation, poisoning American Christianity's understanding of suffering, discipleship, and the very nature of God himself. It has produced a generation of believers who evaluate God's love based on their circumstances, who view faith as a transaction rather than a relationship, and who know nothing about the cost of following Christ.

The Theological Foundation of Heresy

The prosperity gospel rests on several fundamental theological errors that contradict the clear teaching of Scripture. Understanding these errors is crucial for recognizing why this teaching is so dangerous and why it represents a complete departure from biblical Christianity.

The Force of Faith Doctrine

Prosperity teachers claim that faith is a spiritual force that believers can use to manipulate the physical world and compel God to grant their desires. According to this teaching, faith operates according to spiritual laws that work automatically when properly applied, similar to physical laws like gravity or magnetism.

Kenneth Copeland, one of the most prominent prosperity preachers, teaches that "faith is a force" and that believers can use this force to create their own reality. He claims that God used faith to create the universe and that believers can use the same force to create health, wealth, and success in their own lives.

This doctrine transforms faith from trust in God's character and promises into a technique for getting what you want from God. It reduces the Creator of the universe to a cosmic vending machine that dispenses blessings when the right spiritual coins are inserted. It makes God subservient to human desires rather than making humans subservient to God's will.

The biblical understanding of faith is radically different. Hebrews 11:1 defines faith as "confidence in what we hope for and assurance about what we do not see." This faith is directed toward God's promises and character, not toward our own desires or circumstances. It trusts God's wisdom even when his ways don't make sense to human understanding.

Biblical faith often leads to suffering rather than prosperity. Hebrews 11 - the great "faith chapter" - describes believers who "were tortured, refusing to be released so that they might gain an even better resurrection. Some faced jeers and flogging, and even chains and imprisonment. They were put to death by stoning; they were sawed in two; they were killed by the sword. They went about in sheepskins and goatskins, destitute, persecuted and mistreated" (Hebrews 11:35-37).

These faithful believers demonstrated the highest form of faith by trusting God even when their circumstances suggested he had abandoned them. There's no indication that they lacked faith and therefore they suffered. The prosperity gospel's "force of faith" doctrine would condemn these heroes of faith as spiritual failures who lacked the knowledge or commitment to claim their blessings.

The Little Gods Doctrine

Many prosperity teachers promote the heretical belief that humans are "little gods" created in God's image with the same creative power and authority that God possesses. This doctrine claims that believers have the right and ability to speak things into existence, command circumstances to change, and exercise dominion over the physical world through their words and faith.

Kenneth Copeland has taught that believers are "gods" with the same nature as God himself. Creflo Dollar has claimed that Christians are "gods" who can exercise the same creative power that God used to create the universe. Joyce Meyer has taught that believers can "call those things that be not as though they were" and create their own reality through positive confession.

This doctrine represents one of the oldest heresies in human history, the same lie that Satan told Eve in the Garden of Eden: "You will be like God" (Genesis 3:5). It appeals to human pride and the desire for control, promising that believers can transcend their human limitations and exercise divine prerogatives.

The biblical teaching about human nature is clear: humans are created in God's image (Genesis 1:27) but remain finite, fallen creatures who are utterly dependent on God's grace for salvation and blessing. The image of God refers to humans' capacity for relationship with God, moral responsibility, and rational thought - not to divine nature or creative power.

Isaiah 55:8-9 establishes the infinite distance between God and humanity: "'For my thoughts are not your thoughts, neither are your ways my ways,' declares the Lord. 'As the heavens are higher than the earth, so are my ways higher than your ways and my thoughts than your thoughts.'" This passage makes clear that humans cannot think God's thoughts or exercise God's power.

The little gods doctrine reduces God to human limitations. It creates a god who can be manipulated, controlled, and commanded by human beings rather than the sovereign Creator who works all things according to his own will and purpose.

The Positive Confession Doctrine

Prosperity teachers claim that believers can create their own reality through "positive confession." This means speaking positive words about their desired circumstances and avoiding negative words that might prevent their blessings from manifesting. This doctrine teaches that words have creative power and that believers can literally speak their desires into existence.

Joel Osteen regularly teaches his congregation to make positive declarations about their future: "I am blessed. I am prosperous. I am successful. I am victorious. I am talented. I am creative. I am wise." According to prosperity theology, these declarations are creative acts that bring about the declared reality.

This teaching transforms prayer from humble petition to divine command. Instead of asking God for his will to be done, believers are taught to declare what they want to happen and expect God to comply. Instead of submitting to God's sovereignty, they're encouraged to exercise their own sovereignty over their circumstances.

The positive confession doctrine also creates tremendous guilt and fear in believers who experience negative circumstances. If words create reality, then any acknowledgment of problems, struggles, or suffering becomes a spiritual failure that prevents God's blessings from manifesting. Believers are taught to deny obvious realities and maintain positive confessions even when their lives are falling apart.

Biblical prayer follows the model that Christ established in the Lord's Prayer: "Your kingdom come, your will be done, on earth as it is in heaven" (Matthew 6:10). This prayer submits human desires to divine will rather than demanding that divine will conform to human desires.

Christ demonstrated proper prayer in the Garden of Gethsemane: "My Father, if it is possible, may this cup be taken from me. Yet not as I will, but as you will" (Matthew 26:39). Even the Son of God submitted his desires to the Father's will rather than commanding circumstances to change according to his preferences.

The Biblical Refutation

The prosperity gospel crumbles under the weight of biblical evidence that directly contradicts its central claims. Scripture consistently teaches that following Christ leads to suffering rather than prosperity, that God's blessings are often spiritual rather than material, and that earthly wealth can actually be a hindrance to spiritual growth.

Christ's Example of Poverty

The most devastating refutation of the prosperity gospel comes from the life and teaching of Jesus Christ himself. If God wants all believers to be wealthy and successful, why did his own Son live in poverty and die as a criminal?

Christ's earthly life was marked by material deprivation from beginning to end. He was born in a stable because his parents couldn't afford proper lodging (Luke 2:7). His family was so poor that they could only afford the minimum sacrifice required for Mary's purification: two doves instead of a lamb (Luke 2:24, Leviticus 12:8).

During his ministry, Christ had no permanent home and depended on the generosity of others for basic necessities. He told a potential follower, "Foxes have dens and birds have nests, but the Son of Man has no place to lay his head" (Matthew 8:20). When he needed to pay the temple tax, he had to perform a miracle to obtain the necessary money (Matthew 17:24-27).

Christ's poverty was intentional and redemptive. Paul explains in 2 Corinthians 8:9: "For you know the grace of our Lord Jesus Christ, that though he was rich, yet for your sake he became poor, so that you through his poverty might become rich." The riches that believers receive through Christ's poverty are spiritual, not material: forgiveness of sins, reconciliation with God, and eternal life.

Prosperity preachers attempt to explain away Christ's poverty by claiming that he was actually wealthy but chose to live simply, or that his poverty was necessary for his redemptive mission but doesn't apply to his followers. These explanations reveal the desperation of trying to reconcile an obviously false doctrine with biblical truth.

If the prosperity gospel were true, Christ would have been the wealthiest, healthiest, most successful person who ever lived. Instead, he was "despised and rejected by mankind, a man of suffering, and familiar with pain" (Isaiah 53:3). His life demonstrates that God's favor isn't measured by material prosperity but by spiritual faithfulness.

The Apostolic Example of Suffering

The apostles, who had the most intimate relationship with Christ and the greatest faith of any believers in history, experienced lives marked by poverty, persecution, and suffering rather than health, wealth, and success. If the prosperity gospel were true, these men should have been the most prosperous people on earth.

Paul's description of apostolic ministry contradicts prosperity theology: "Up to this moment we have become the scum of the earth, the garbage of the world. To this very hour we go hungry and thirsty, we are in rags, we are brutally treated, we are homeless. We work hard with our own hands. When we are cursed, we bless; when we are persecuted, we endure it; when we are slandered, we answer kindly" (1 Corinthians 4:13-13).

Paul's catalog of sufferings in 2 Corinthians 11:23-28 reads like a prosperity preacher's nightmare: "I have worked much harder, been in prison more frequently, been flogged more severely, and been exposed to death again and again. Five times I received from the Jews the forty lashes minus one. Three times I was beaten with rods, once I was pelted with stones, three times I was shipwrecked, I spent a night and a day in the open sea, I have been constantly on the move. I have been in danger from rivers, in danger from bandits, in danger from my fellow Jews, in danger from Gentiles; in danger in the city, in danger in the country, in danger at sea; and in danger from false believers. I have labored and toiled and have often gone without sleep; I have known hunger and thirst and have often gone without food; I have been cold and naked. Besides everything else, I face daily the pressure of my concern for all the churches."

According to prosperity theology, Paul's sufferings indicate spiritual failure, insufficient faith, or inadequate knowledge of God's promises. But Paul presents these sufferings as credentials of authentic apostolic ministry and evidence of God's favor rather than his displeasure.

The other apostles experienced similar fates. James was executed by Herod (Acts 12:2). Peter was crucified upside down. Thomas was speared to death in India. Most of the apostles died as martyrs, and none of them accumulated material wealth or achieved worldly success.

These men had walked with Christ, witnessed his miracles, received direct revelation from God, and possessed faith that could move mountains. If anyone should have been able to claim prosperity through faith, it was the apostles. Their lives of suffering and sacrifice demonstrate that God's favor often manifests through trials rather than triumphs.

The Rich Young Ruler

Christ's encounter with the rich young ruler provides perhaps the clearest refutation of prosperity theology in all of Scripture. This man had everything that prosperity preachers promise, including, youth, wealth, moral respectability, and apparent spiritual interest. According to prosperity theology, his material success should have indicated God's blessing and spiritual maturity.

But Christ's response revealed the spiritual danger of material prosperity: "Jesus answered, 'If you want to be perfect, go, sell your possessions and give to the poor, and you will have treasure in heaven. Then come and follow me.' When the young man heard this, he went away sad, because he had great wealth" (Matthew 19:21-22).

Christ didn't promise the young man greater wealth if he followed him. He demanded that he abandon his wealth entirely. The man's riches weren't a sign of God's blessing but a barrier to spiritual growth that prevented him from following Christ.

Christ's commentary on this encounter directly contradicts prosperity theology: "Truly I tell you, it is hard for someone who is rich to enter the kingdom of heaven. Again I tell you, it is easier for a camel to go through the eye of a needle than for someone who is rich to enter the kingdom of God" (Matthew 19:23-24).

Prosperity preachers have developed elaborate explanations to avoid the obvious meaning of this passage. Some claim that the "eye of the needle" was a narrow gate in Jerusalem that camels could pass through with difficulty. Others argue that Christ was only addressing the specific problem of this particular rich man, not making a general statement about wealth.

These interpretations ignore the disciples' shocked response: "When the disciples heard this, they were greatly astonished and asked, 'Who then can be saved?'" (Matthew 19:25). The disciples understood Christ to be making a general statement about the spiritual danger of wealth, not addressing a unique situation.

Christ's teaching about wealth consistently emphasizes its spiritual dangers rather than its divine benefits. He warned that "you cannot serve both God and money" (Matthew 6:24) and told his followers not to "store up for yourselves treasures on earth" but to "store up for yourselves treasures in heaven" (Matthew 6:19-20).

The Devastating Practical Consequences

The prosperity gospel destroys lives. The practical consequences of this false teaching extend far beyond the obvious financial exploitation to include spiritual, emotional, and relational devastation that affects entire families and communities.

Financial Exploitation and Ruin

The most visible consequence of prosperity teaching is the systematic financial exploitation of vulnerable people who can least afford to lose money. Prosperity preachers target the poor, the sick, the elderly, and the desperate with promises that financial giving will result in miraculous returns on their "seed offerings."

These false teachers live in mansions, fly in private jets, and wear expensive clothing while encouraging their followers to send money they can't afford to lose. Kenneth Copeland owns multiple private jets and lives in a $6 million mansion. Creflo Dollar attempted to raise $65 million from his followers to purchase a luxury jet. Joel Osteen lives in a $10.5 million mansion in the most exclusive area of Houston.

The contrast between the prosperity preachers' lavish lifestyles and their followers' financial struggles reveals the true nature of this movement. These men aren't teaching biblical principles of steward-ship and generosity - they're operating sophisticated financial schemes that transfer wealth from the poor to the rich under the guise of spiritual ministry.

The financial damage extends beyond individual losses to include families destroyed by bankruptcy, retirement savings depleted by false promises, and children deprived of basic necessities because their parents sent money to prosperity preachers. The elderly are particularly vulnerable to these schemes, often giving away their life savings in desperate attempts to secure healing or financial break-through.

Prosperity preachers defend their wealth by claiming that God has blessed them because of their great faith, but their lifestyles directly contradict Christ's teaching about money and ministry. Christ told his disciples not to take money, extra clothing, or even a traveler's bag when he sent them out to preach (Matthew 10:9-10). Paul worked as a tentmaker to support his ministry rather than living off the contribu-tions of his converts (Acts 18:3).

The Theology of Victim Blaming

Perhaps the most cruel aspect of prosperity theology is its system-atic blaming of victims for their own suffering. According to this teaching, sickness indicates insufficient faith, poverty reveals spiritual failure, and tragedy results from negative confession or hidden sin.

This victim-blaming theology creates tremendous guilt and shame in believers who experience normal human difficulties. Cancer patients are told that their disease results from lack of faith. Unemployed workers are blamed for not claiming their prosperity with sufficient conviction. Parents who lose children are accused of speaking negative words that prevented God's protection from manifesting.

The psychological damage of this teaching is immense. Instead of receiving comfort and support during difficult times, prosperity gospel adherents face additional condemnation from their religious community. They're taught that admitting problems or seeking help demonstrates spiritual weakness that will prevent their breakthrough from occurring.

This theology also prevents believers from developing the spiritual maturity that comes through suffering. Instead of learning to trust God during trials, they're taught to deny the reality of their circumstances and maintain positive confessions regardless of their actual situation. This produces shallow, immature believers who lack the spiritual resources necessary to handle life's inevitable difficulties.

The Bible presents a radically different perspective on suffering. Job's friends made the same mistake as prosperity preachers by assuming that Job's suffering indicated spiritual failure and that his restoration depended on identifying and confessing his hidden sins. But God condemned their theology and vindicated Job's righteousness despite his suffering.

Christ himself warned that his followers would experience suffering in this world: "I have told you these things, so that in me you may have peace. In this world you will have trouble. But take heart! I have overcome the world" (John 16:33). This promised contradicts prosperity theology's claim that faith eliminates suffering and guarantees earthly blessing.

The apostles understood that suffering was normal for Christians rather than evidence of spiritual failure. Paul wrote: "We must go through many hardships to enter the kingdom of God" (Acts 14:22). Peter encouraged believers: "Dear friends, do not be surprised at the fiery ordeal that has come on you to test you, as though something strange were happening to you. But rejoice inasmuch as you participate in the sufferings of Christ, so that you may be overjoyed when his glory is revealed" (1 Peter 4:12-13).

These passages present suffering as a normal part of Christian experience that can actually indicate spiritual maturity rather than spiritual failure. The prosperity gospel's victim-blaming theology turns biblical truth upside down by making suffering evidence of sin rather than evidence of faithfulness.

THE CELEBRITY PASTOR INDUSTRIAL COMPLEX

The prosperity gospel has created a celebrity pastor culture that treats church leaders like entertainment figures rather than spiritual shepherds. These celebrity pastors build personal brands, accumulate massive wealth, and live lifestyles that directly contradict Christ's teaching about Christian leadership and material possessions. Even in smaller churches, the pastor is seen as some kind of minor rockstar, leading to a lot of problems within the church and without.

The Megachurch Business Model

Modern prosperity preachers operate megachurches that function more like entertainment corporations than biblical churches. These operations require massive facilities, professional staff, sophisticated marketing campaigns, and revenue streams that dwarf traditional church budgets.

Joel Osteen's Lakewood Church in Houston occupies a former NBA arena that seats 16,800 people and cost $105 million to renovate. The church generates millions of dollars annually through offerings, book sales, speaking fees, and media licensing deals. Osteen himself has a net worth estimated at $100 million and lives in a $10.5 million mansion.

Kenneth Copeland Ministries operates from a 1,500-acre campus in Texas that includes multiple buildings, a private airstrip, and hangar facilities for Copeland's fleet of private jets. Copeland's personal net worth is estimated at $300 million, and he has defended his luxury lifestyle by claiming that commercial airlines are filled with "demons" that would interfere with his ministry.

Creflo Dollar attempted to raise $65 million from his followers to purchase a Gulfstream G650 jet, claiming that his current aircraft was too old and small for international ministry. When public criticism forced him to abandon the campaign, he later acquired the jet through other means while maintaining that God wanted him to have the best transportation available.

These examples reveal the complete inversion of biblical priorities that characterizes the prosperity gospel movement. Instead of shepherds who sacrifice for their flocks, these men are entrepreneurs who exploit their followers for personal gain. Instead of following Christ's example of poverty and service, they accumulate wealth and live in luxury while their followers struggle financially.

The Contradiction of Christ's Example

The lifestyle of prosperity preachers creates an insurmountable theological problem: how can they claim to follow Jesus Christ while living in ways that directly contradict his example and teaching? Christ lived in poverty, owned no property, and warned repeatedly about the spiritual dangers of wealth.

When a rich young ruler asked Christ what he must do to inherit eternal life, Christ told him to "sell everything you have and give to the poor, and you will have treasure in heaven. Then come, follow me" (Luke 18:22). If prosperity preachers truly believed their own teaching about following Christ, they would sell their mansions, give away their private jets, and live simply while using their resources to help the poor.

Instead, they develop elaborate theological justifications for their wealth. They claim that God wants them to live in prosperity as an example of his blessing, that their wealth enables greater ministry effectiveness, or that their success proves the validity of their teaching. These justifications reveal the depth of their self-deception and their distance from biblical Christianity.

Christ's warning about the impossibility of serving both God and money (Matthew 6:24) applies directly to prosperity preachers who have clearly chosen money over God while maintaining religious vocabulary and Christian branding. Their lifestyles demonstrate that they serve money while using God as a means to acquire more wealth.

The Spiritual Abuse of Authority

Prosperity preachers abuse their spiritual authority by using their positions as religious leaders to manipulate vulnerable people into giving money they cannot afford to lose. This abuse is particularly cruel because it targets people who are desperate for help and willing to trust religious leaders who claim to speak for God.

These false teachers use sophisticated psychological manipulation techniques to extract money from their followers. They create artificial urgency by claiming that God has given them specific instructions about offerings that must be received immediately. They promise miraculous returns on "seed offerings" that will multiply back to the giver. They use guilt and fear to pressure people into giving by suggesting that failure to give indicates lack of faith or disobedience to God.

The most vulnerable populations of the elderly, the sick, the poor, and the desperate, are specifically targeted by these manipulation techniques. Elderly people on fixed incomes are encouraged to give their Social Security checks as "seed offerings." Sick people are told that their healing depends on their financial giving. Poor people are promised that giving money they don't have will break the "spirit of poverty" that keeps them in financial bondage.

This systematic exploitation of vulnerable people represents spiritual abuse of the worst kind. These preachers use their religious authority and their followers' trust to enrich themselves while impoverishing the very people they claim to serve. They turn the Gospel into a get-rich-quick scheme that benefits only the preachers who promote it.

The Cycle of False Hope and Crushing Disappointment

Prosperity teaching creates a cycle of false hope followed by crushing disappointment that repeats endlessly in the lives of believers who embrace this false gospel. People are taught to expect miraculous financial breakthroughs, supernatural healing, and material blessings that rarely materialize despite their faithful giving and positive confession.

When the promised blessings don't arrive, believers are told they need to give more money, confess more positively, or have greater faith. This creates a cycle where failure to receive promised blessings is always blamed on the believer rather than on the false promises themselves. People spend years chasing breakthroughs that never come while impoverishing themselves through continued giving to prosperity ministries.

The psychological damage of this cycle is immense. Believers develop learned helplessness as they repeatedly fail to achieve the results that prosperity teaching promises. They begin to question their own faith, their relationship with God, and their worth as human beings. Many eventually abandon Christianity entirely, concluding that if the prosperity gospel is false, then all Christianity must be false.

Others develop deep spiritual wounds that make it difficult for them to trust God, trust church leaders, or believe biblical promises about God's love and care. They become cynical about Christianity and suspicious of all religious teaching because they've been so thoroughly deceived by false promises made in God's name.

The Destruction of Biblical Faith

The prosperity gospel destroys biblical faith by replacing trust in God's character with expectation of material blessing. Biblical faith trusts God regardless of circumstances, believing that he is good even when life is difficult. Prosperity gospel faith depends on favorable circumstances and collapses when expected blessings don't materialize.

This false faith cannot survive the normal trials and difficulties that characterize life in a fallen world. When prosperity believers face serious illness, financial hardship, or family tragedy, their faith crumbles because it was built on false promises rather than on God's unchanging character and eternal purposes.

The book of Hebrews describes biblical faith through examples of believers who trusted God despite adverse circumstances: "All these people were still living by faith when they died. They did not receive the things promised; they only saw them and welcomed them from a distance, admitting that they were foreigners and strangers on earth" (Hebrews 11:13).

This passage describes faith that persists despite unfulfilled earthly expectations because it's focused on eternal rather than temporal promises. Prosperity gospel faith lacks this eternal perspective and therefore cannot survive temporal disappointments.

The Generational Impact

The prosperity gospel's destructive effects extend beyond individual believers to impact entire families and communities. Children raised in prosperity gospel environments often develop distorted understandings of God, faith, and the Christian life that affect their spiritual development for decades.

These children learn to evaluate God's love based on material circumstances rather than on his character revealed in Scripture. They develop transactional relationships with God where prayer becomes a means of getting things rather than communion with their Creator. They learn to measure spiritual success by material prosperity rather than by growth in holiness and love.

When these children experience normal life difficulties - academic struggles, relationship problems, career setbacks - they often conclude that God doesn't love them or that they lack sufficient faith. The prosperity gospel's false promises create unrealistic expectations that set children up for spiritual failure and disillusionment.

Many children from prosperity gospel families eventually reject Christianity entirely because they cannot reconcile the false promises they were taught with the reality of life in a fallen world. Others spend years recovering from the spiritual damage caused by false teaching and learning to understand biblical Christianity for the first time.

THE BIBLICAL ALTERNATIVE: TRUE PROSPERITY

The New Testament consistently describes the true riches that believers possess in Christ -asspiritual blessings that far exceed any material wealth. Paul writes: "Praise be to the God and Father of our Lord Jesus Christ, who has blessed us in the heavenly realms with every spiritual blessing in Christ" (Ephesians 1:3).

These spiritual blessings include adoption as God's children, forgiveness of sins, the indwelling Holy Spirit, eternal life, and the promise of resurrection. These blessings have infinite value and cannot be lost through economic downturns, health problems, or other earthly difficulties.

Peter describes believers as having "an inheritance that can never perish, spoil or fade. This inheritance is kept in heaven for you" (1 Peter 1:4). This eternal inheritance provides security and hope that no earthly prosperity can match because it depends on God's faithfulness rather than human circumstances.

The prosperity gospel's focus on temporal blessings distracts believers from these eternal riches and creates dissatisfaction with the spiritual wealth they already possess in Christ. It teaches people to desire lesser things while ignoring the greater things that God has already provided.

Contentment and Godliness

Paul provides the biblical perspective on material prosperity in his letter to Timothy: "But godliness with contentment is great gain. For we brought nothing into the world, and we can take nothing out of it. But if we have food and clothing, we will be content with that. Those who want to get rich fall into temptation and a trap and into many foolish and harmful desires that plunge people into ruin and destruction" (1 Timothy 6:6-9).

This passage presents contentment with basic necessities as "great gain" while warning about the spiritual dangers of desiring wealth. The prosperity gospel inverts this teaching by presenting material wealth as great gain while ignoring the spiritual dangers that accompany the pursuit of riches.

Paul's personal example demonstrates this principle in practice. He wrote: "I know what it is to be in need, and I know what it is to have plenty. I have learned the secret of being content in any and every situation, whether well fed or hungry, whether living in plenty or in want. I can do all this through him who gives me strength" (Philippians 4:12-13).

This passage, often misquoted by prosperity preachers to support their false promises, actually teaches contentment in both prosperity and poverty rather than expectation of constant material blessing. Paul's strength came from Christ's presence rather than from favorable circumstances.

The Eternal Perspective

Biblical prosperity maintains an eternal perspective that values heavenly treasure over earthly wealth. Christ taught his followers: "Do not store up for yourselves treasures on earth, where moths and vermin destroy, and where thieves break in and steal. But store up for yourselves treasures in heaven, where moths and vermin do not destroy, and where thieves do not break in and steal. For where your treasure is, there your heart will be also" (Matthew 6:19-21).

This teaching again contradicts prosperity gospel emphasis on accumulating earthly wealth and material possessions. Christ calls his followers to prioritize eternal values over temporal concerns and to find their security in heavenly rather than earthly treasure.

The prosperity gospel's promise of earthly blessing distracts believers from the eternal perspective that Christ taught and prevents them from storing up treasures in heaven. It creates earthly-minded Christians who are more concerned with temporal comfort than eternal significance.

The true prosperity that God offers his people includes spiritual blessings that begin in this life and continue throughout eternity, contentment that doesn't depend on circumstances, and the eternal perspective that values heavenly treasure over earthly wealth. This biblical prosperity provides lasting satisfaction and genuine security that the false promises of the prosperity gospel can never deliver.

The prosperity gospel heresy represents one of the most destructive false teachings in the history of Christianity because it corrupts the Gospel itself while appearing to offer God's blessing. Churches and believers who want to avoid this deception must return to biblical teaching about suffering, contentment, and the true riches that believers possess in Christ. Only then can they experience the genuine prosperity that comes from knowing God and walking in his ways rather than chasing the false promises of health and wealth preachers who have turned the Gospel into a get-rich-quick scheme.

5

SACRAMENTAL STARVATION - ABANDONING SACRED TRADITIONS

THE REFORMATION BEGAN WITH LEGITIMATE CONCERNS ABOUT corruption in the Catholic Church, but as the centuries went on, many denominations threw out the baby with the bathwater. They abandoned the sacramental life that had sustained Christians for over 1,500 years, leaving their followers spiritually malnourished and disconnected from the rhythms of grace that God designed for his people.

This sacramental starvation has produced generations of modern Christians who know nothing about the sacred mysteries that transform ordinary elements into vehicles of divine grace. They've been taught that sacraments are merely symbols, that rituals are empty formalism, and that individual Bible reading can replace the communal worship practices that shaped Christian civilization for millennia. But why would modern Christians presume that they know better than Christians for the first thousand and more years after Christ?

The consequences of this abandonment extend far beyond theological differences to include the practical spiritual poverty that characterizes much of American Christianity today. Without sacramental anchors, Modern churches have drifted into entertainment, therapy, and social activism because they lack the sacred center that gives meaning to all other church activities.

Meanwhile, the Catholic, Orthodox, Anglican, and some Lutheran churches have preserved these ancient practices, maintaining an unbroken connection to the apostolic tradition that churches severed in their rush to embrace "Scripture alone." This preservation hasn't been perfect. However, it has maintained the sacramental framework that provides structure, meaning, and grace to the Christian life.

Understanding what Christianity lost requires examining what the sacraments actually are, where they came from, and why they matter for Christian spiritual development. Only then can we appreciate the magnitude of what was abandoned and why many churches today feel spiritually hollow despite their biblical emphasis.

The Biblical and Historical Foundation of Sacraments

The sacramental system didn't emerge from medieval superstition or clerical power-grabbing like many modern Christians believe. It developed from careful reflection on biblical teaching and apostolic practice and the rituals often stem from early church origins. The early church recognized that God works through physical means to convey spiritual grace, using material elements as vehicles for divine blessing in ways that honor both the spiritual and physical aspects of human nature.

Christ established this sacramental principle through his incarnation. The eternal Word became flesh (John 1:14), demonstrating that God doesn't despise material creation but uses it as a means of revelation and redemption. If God could become man to save humanity, then bread and wine can become vehicles of grace, water can convey spiritual cleansing, and oil can channel divine healing.

The New Testament records Christ's institution of at least two sacraments that virtually all Christian traditions recognize: baptism and communion. But careful examination of Scripture reveals additional sacramental practices that the apostolic church observed and that the Catholic Church later systematized into seven sacraments.

Baptism: The Gateway Sacrament

Christ's command to baptize is unambiguous: "Therefore go and make disciples of all nations, baptizing them in the name of the Father and of the Son and of the Holy Spirit" (Matthew 28:19). This isn't merely a symbolic act or public declaration - it's a sacramental participation in Christ's death and resurrection that actually accomplishes spiritual transformation.

Paul's explanation of baptism in Romans 6:3-4 reveals its sacramental nature: "Or don't you know that all of us who were baptized into Christ Jesus were baptized into his death? We were therefore buried with him through baptism into death in order that, just as Christ was raised from the dead through the glory of the Father, we too may live a new life."

This passage describes baptism as more than symbolism - it's actual participation in Christ's death and resurrection. The believer doesn't just symbolically die to sin; he actually dies to sin through the sacramental act of baptism. The water doesn't just represent cleansing; it actually conveys the cleansing power of Christ's blood.

The early church understood baptism's sacramental efficacy. Peter declared on Pentecost: "Repent and be baptized, every one of you, in the name of Jesus Christ for the forgiveness of your sins. And you will receive the gift of the Holy Spirit" (Acts 2:38). Baptism doesn't just symbolize forgiveness - it actually conveys forgiveness and the gift of the Holy Spirit.

Most churches have retained baptism but reduced it to a symbolic act that declares what God has already done rather than a sacramental act through which God actually works. This reduction eliminates the mystery and power of the sacrament, turning it into a human testimony rather than a divine action.

The Eucharist: The Central Sacrament

Christ's institution of the Eucharist at the Last Supper provides the clearest example of sacramental theology in Scripture. His words - "This is my body" and "This is my blood" (Matthew 26:26-28) - indicate real presence rather than mere symbolism, actual participation in his sacrifice rather than simple remembrance.

John 6:53-56 reinforces the reality of Christ's presence in the Eucharist: "Jesus said to them, 'Very truly I tell you, unless you eat the flesh of the Son of Man and drink his blood, you have no life in you. Whoever eats my flesh and drinks my blood has eternal life, and I will raise them up at the last day. For my flesh is real food and my blood is real drink. Whoever eats my flesh and drinks my blood remains in me, and I in them.'"

This passage describes actual spiritual nourishment through consuming Christ's body and blood, not symbolic remembrance of his sacrifice. The language is sacramental with physical elements (bread and wine) becoming vehicles for spiritual reality (Christ's body and blood) that provide actual spiritual nourishment to believers.

Paul's warning about unworthy reception of communion confirms its sacramental nature: "So then, whoever eats the bread or drinks the cup of the Lord in an unworthy manner will be guilty of sinning against the body and blood of the Lord. Everyone ought to examine themselves before they eat of the bread and drink from the cup. For those who eat and drink without discerning the body of Christ eat and drink judgment on themselves" (1 Corinthians 11:27-29).

If communion were merely symbolic, unworthy reception couldn't bring judgment. The fact that improper reception has spiritual consequences demonstrates that something real happens in the sacrament. Christ is actually present in the bread and wine, making reverent reception essential.

Most churches have reduced communion to a memorial meal that helps believers remember Christ's sacrifice. This reduction eliminates the real presence of Christ and turns the sacrament into a human act of remembrance rather than a divine act of grace. The result is communion services that feel more like history lessons than encounters with the living Christ.

The Five Additional Sacraments

The Catholic Church recognizes five additional sacraments that have biblical foundations and apostolic origins, even though churches have largely abandoned them. Understanding these sacraments reveals the comprehensive sacramental system that once provided structure and meaning to the entire Christian life.

Confirmation builds on baptism by providing the gifts of the

Holy Spirit necessary for mature Christian living. The apostles practiced this sacrament when they laid hands on new believers to receive the Holy Spirit (Acts 8:14-17, Acts 19:5-6). This sacrament marks the transition from childhood faith to adult commitment and provides spiritual strength for the challenges of Christian discipleship.

Confession provides the means for post-baptismal forgiveness that Christ established when he gave the apostles authority to forgive sins: "If you forgive anyone's sins, their sins are forgiven; if you do not forgive them, they are not forgiven" (John 20:23). This sacrament offers the assurance of forgiveness and the spiritual direction necessary for growth in holiness.

Marriage elevates the natural institution of marriage to a sacramental level that reflects Christ's relationship with the church. Paul's teaching in Ephesians 5:31-32 reveals marriage's sacramental nature: "For this reason a man will leave his father and mother and be united to his wife, and the two will become one flesh. This is a profound mystery—but I am talking about Christ and the church."

Holy Orders provides the sacramental foundation for church leadership through the laying on of hands that the apostles practiced (1 Timothy 4:14, 2 Timothy 1:6). This sacrament doesn't just recognize natural leadership ability but actually confers the spiritual authority necessary for pastoral ministry.

Anointing of the Sick offers spiritual and physical healing through the prayer and anointing that James describes: "Is anyone among you sick? Let them call the elders of the church to pray over them and anoint them with oil in the name of the Lord. And the prayer offered in faith will make the sick person well; the Lord will raise them up. If they have sinned, they will be forgiven" (James 5:14-15).

These five sacraments, combined with baptism and Eucharist, provide a comprehensive system of grace that addresses every stage and challenge of Christian life. From birth to death, from conversion to marriage to ordination to final illness, the sacraments offer divine grace through physical means that honor both the spiritual and material aspects of human existence.

The Loss of Sacramental Rhythm

The seven sacraments provided a rhythm of grace that structured the entire Christian life around encounters with God through physical means. This rhythm began with baptism in infancy, continued through confirmation in adolescence, marriage or ordination in young adulthood, regular confession and communion throughout life, and concluded with anointing of the sick before death.

This sacramental rhythm meant that no stage of life lacked divine grace, no major transition occurred without spiritual support, and no crisis arose without sacramental resources for healing and strength. The Christian life was a communal journey marked by regular encounters with God through the sacramental system.

Modern churches that abandoned this rhythm left their members spiritually adrift during major life transitions. Without confirmation, young people lack a clear rite of passage into adult faith. Without sacramental marriage, couples miss the spiritual foundation that transforms natural love into supernatural grace. Without confession, believers struggle with guilt and spiritual direction. Without anointing of the sick, the dying face their final moments without sacramental comfort.

The absence of sacramental rhythm has contributed to the spiritual shallowness that characterizes much of American Christianity. Without regular encounters with divine grace through physical means, believers develop a purely intellectual or emotional relationship with God that lacks the depth and stability that sacramental practice provides.

The Loss of Sacramental Community

The sacramental system created a community bound together by shared participation in divine grace rather than just shared beliefs or social connections. When believers received the same sacraments, participated in the same liturgical calendar, and experienced the same rhythm of grace, they developed bonds that transcended individual preferences or personality differences.

This sacramental community provided stability during times of change, support during times of crisis, and continuity across generations. Children grew up participating in the same sacramental life as their parents and grandparents, creating a sense of connection to the broader Christian tradition that extended back to the apostles themselves.

Modern churches that abandoned sacramental community often struggle to maintain unity and continuity. Without shared sacramental practices, these churches tend to fragment along theological, cultural, or generational lines. They lack the common foundation that sacramental participation provides, making them vulnerable to division and drift.

The consumer mentality that characterizes much of American Christianity partly results from the loss of sacramental community. When churches become voluntary associations based on personal preference rather than sacramental communities bound by divine grace, believers naturally approach them like consumers shopping for services rather than pilgrims seeking transformation.

The Loss of Sacramental Mystery

The sacramental system preserved the mystery and transcendence that characterize authentic encounters with God. When believers participated in sacraments, they experienced divine grace working through physical means in ways that couldn't be fully explained or manipulated.

This sacramental mystery cultivated humility, reverence, and awe that protected believers from the pride and presumption that often characterize purely intellectual approaches to faith. Believers who regularly encountered God through sacraments understood that Christianity required participation in divine mysteries that transformed human nature itself.

Churches that abandoned sacramental mystery often replaced it with either intellectual complexity or emotional manipulation. Some developed elaborate theological systems that made faith primarily a matter of correct understanding. Others created emotional experiences designed to generate feelings of spiritual connection. Both approaches lack the authentic mystery that sacramental participation provides.

The absence of sacramental mystery has contributed to the entertainment mentality that plagues many churches. When worship becomes primarily about human understanding or human emotion rather than divine mystery, it naturally evolves toward whatever generates the strongest intellectual or emotional response. We can see this often indulges in entertainment, therapy, or political activism.

The Catholic And Orthodox Preservation of Sacred Tradition

While churches were abandoning sacramental life, the Catholic and Orthodox Churches maintained its commitment to the seven sacraments and the liturgical traditions that had developed around them. This preservation wasn't perfect, but it maintained the sacramental framework that provides structure and meaning to Christian worship.

The Mass as Central Worship

The Mass preserves the ancient Christian understanding of worship as primarily sacramental rather than educational or emotional. The Mass centers on the Eucharist as the real presence of Christ in bread and wine with the preaching and music taking secondary roles. This is reversed in modern churches, many of which don't offer communion at all at regular services, ignoring Christ's commands.

This sacramental focus means that every Mass provides an authentic encounter with Christ regardless of the priest's preaching ability, the quality of the music, or the friendliness of the congregation. The Mass doesn't depend on human performance for its spiritual value because its center is divine action rather than human activity.

Modern American worship services that abandoned sacramental focus often become dependent on human performance for their spiritual impact. If the preaching is poor, the music is bad, or the fellowship is unfriendly, the service feels spiritually empty because it lacks a sacramental center that provides meaning independent of human effort.

The Mass also preserves the liturgical calendar that structures Christian worship around the major events of salvation history including Advent, Christmas, Epiphany, Lent, Easter, and Pentecost.

This calendar ensures that the full scope of Christian truth is celebrated annually rather than depending on the pastor's personal interests or current events for worship themes. While churches all recognize Easter and Christmas, there's a lot more to the liturgical year than many acknowledge as they abandon his tory and tradition.

Confession and Spiritual Direction

Perhaps the most controversial sacrament in modern times is the act of confession. The mere idea of confessing one's sins is extremely uncomfortable, and therefore ignored by many modern church-goers as they will react angrily, "That's between me and God!"

The Catholic Church's preservation of the sacrament of confession, by contrast, provides believers with regular opportunities for spiritual cleansing, guidance, and growth that most modern churches lack. Confession offers not just forgiveness but also spiritual direction from trained clergy who can help believers identify patterns of sin and develop strategies for spiritual growth. This is true pastoral care and shepherding of a flock that can't be attained easily without assistance and outside reflection.

The anonymity and formality of sacramental confession also provide psychological benefits that informal counseling often lacks. Believers can confess their worst sins without fear of social consequences while receiving authoritative assurance of forgiveness that human counselors cannot provide.

Modern churches have attempted to replace confession with various forms of counseling, accountability groups, and pastoral care, but these alternatives lack the sacramental authority and spiritual efficacy that formal confession provides. They depend on human wisdom and emotional support rather than divine grace and sacramental power.

The Modern Overemphasis on Faith Alone

The doctrine of "sola fide," faith alone, began as a necessary correction to medieval Catholic teaching that had become confused about the relationship between faith and works in salvation. The Reformers rightly emphasized that salvation comes through faith in Christ rather than through human effort or religious performance.

Many, however, took it to extremes to invalidate certain sacraments rather than rightly chastise the clergy that were abusing their positions for personal gain, a sin they indulged in rather than the system being flawed.

As this idea spread over generations, many modern churches have taken this doctrine to further extremes that contradict other biblical teachings about the necessity of good works in the Christian life. They've created a false dichotomy between faith and works that has produced generations of believers who think that faith requires no corresponding action and that works play no role in Christian living.

THE BIBLICAL BALANCE OF FAITH AND WORKS

Scripture teaches both that salvation comes through faith alone and that genuine faith always produces good works. These aren't contradictory teachings but complementary truths that describe different aspects of the same spiritual reality.

Paul's teaching in Ephesians 2:8-10 provides the perfect balance: "For it is by grace you have been saved, through faith—and this is not from yourselves, it is the gift of God—not by works, so that no one can boast. For we are God's handiwork, created in Christ Jesus to do good works, which God prepared in advance for us to do."

This passage establishes that salvation comes through grace alone, received through faith alone, not through human works. But it immediately explains that saved believers are "created in Christ Jesus to do good works" that God has prepared for them. Salvation doesn't depend on works, but salvation always produces works. If those works are not there, then there is also likely not salvation.

James reinforces this balance with his famous declaration: "Faith by itself, if it is not accompanied by action, is dead" (James 2:17). He continues: "Show me your faith without deeds, and I will show you my faith by my deeds" (James 2:18). James isn't contradicting Paul's teaching about salvation by faith alone—he's explaining that genuine saving faith always manifests itself through good works.

Newer Christians and their overemphasis on "faith alone" has created a generation of believers who think that faith requires no corresponding action and that works play no role in the Christian life. It demonstrates that their faith, in fact, does not exist at all because they're unwilling to make the changes required to be follower of Christ. They've misunderstood the Reformation principle to mean that Christians can live however they want as long as they have faith, ignoring the biblical teaching that genuine faith transforms behavior.

The Catholic Understanding of Faith and Works

The Catholic Church has maintained a more balanced understanding of the relationship between faith and works that avoids both the error of salvation by works and the error of faith without works. Catholic teaching recognizes that salvation comes through God's grace received through faith, but it also emphasizes that this faith must be living faith that expresses itself through love and good works.

The Council of Trent, responding to accusations that Catholics taught salvation by works, clarified that "we are therefore said to be justified by faith because faith is the beginning of human salvation, the foundation, and the root of all justification; without which it is impossible to please God." But the Council also taught that this justifying faith must be accompanied by hope and love, and that it grows through good works performed in God's grace.

This understanding avoids the tendency to separate faith from works while maintaining the biblical truth that salvation comes through God's grace rather than human effort. It recognizes that faith, hope, and love work together in the process of salvation and that good works are both the fruit of salvation and the means by which salvation is worked out in the believer's life.

The Catholic emphasis on the necessity of good works completes the idea of faith by recognizing that genuine faith always produces the works that God has prepared for believers to do.

The Sacramental Life as Faith in Action

The Catholic sacramental system provides the perfect example of how faith and works operate together in the Christian life. The sacraments require both faith and action—believers must have faith in

God's promises while also participating in the physical actions that God has established as means of grace.

Baptism illustrates this principle clearly. The sacrament requires faith in Christ's death and resurrection, but it also requires the physical action of water baptism. The faith without the action would be incomplete, and the action without faith would be meaningless. Together, they constitute the sacramental reality through which God conveys grace.

The same principle applies to all the sacraments. Communion requires faith in Christ's real presence, but it also requires the physical action of receiving the consecrated bread and wine. Confession requires faith in God's forgiveness, but it also requires the action of confessing sins to a priest. Marriage requires faith in God's design for matrimony, but it also requires the action of making vows before the church.

This sacramental understanding demonstrates how faith and works operate together in authentic Christian living. Faith provides the spiritual foundation, but works provide the concrete expression through which faith becomes real and effective in the believer's life.

Churches that have abandoned sacramental life often struggle to maintain this balance between faith and works. Without concrete actions through which faith can be expressed and strengthened, believers often develop a purely intellectual or emotional relationship with God that lacks the depth and stability that sacramental practice provides.

THE LOSS OF SPIRITUAL DISCIPLINE

The overemphasis on faith alone has contributed to the abandonment of spiritual disciplines that have sustained Christians for centuries. Many churches teach that spiritual disciplines like fasting, prayer, meditation, and pilgrimage are "works righteousness" that distract from simple faith in Christ.

This abandonment has produced spiritually weak believers who lack the disciplines necessary for spiritual growth and maturity. They know how to attend church services and read their Bibles, but they don't know how to fast, pray the hours, examine their consciences, or engage in the other practices that develop spiritual strength and character.

The Monastic Tradition

The Catholic Church has preserved the monastic tradition that demonstrates the highest expression of Christian discipleship through lives devoted entirely to prayer, work, and service. Monasteries and convents provide examples of what Christian life looks like when it's organized around spiritual rather than material priorities.

The monastic vows of poverty, chastity, and obedience represent the complete surrender to God that Christ called his followers to embrace. These vows aren't arbitrary restrictions but spiritual disciplines that free believers from the worldly attachments that prevent spiritual growth.

Modern American churches that rejected monasticism lost this witness to the radical demands of Christian discipleship. Without monastic communities to demonstrate what complete devotion to God looks like, Christianity often settles for a comfortable middle-class lifestyle that accommodates worldly values rather than challenging them.

The monastic tradition also preserved many of the spiritual disciplines that sustained Christian spirituality for centuries. Monks and nuns developed sophisticated practices of prayer, meditation, spiritual direction, and contemplation that enabled deep communion with God and profound spiritual transformation.

Modern churches that abandoned these traditions often lack the spiritual resources necessary to help believers grow beyond basic conversion and church attendance. They can lead people to faith in Christ, but they struggle to help them develop the spiritual maturity that comes through disciplined spiritual practice.

THE RECOVERY OF SACRAMENTAL DEPTH

Churches that want to recover spiritual depth and authenticity must reconsider their relationship to sacramental life and spiritual discipline. This doesn't necessarily require converting to Catholicism, but it does require acknowledging what was lost in the rejection of Catholic practices and working to recover the spiritual riches that were abandoned.

Rediscovering the Real Presence

Many churches could benefit from rediscovering the reality of Christ's presence in communion rather than treating it as merely symbolic remembrance.

This rediscovery would transform communion from a quarterly memorial service into a regular encounter with the living Christ that provides spiritual nourishment and strength. It would also restore the reverence and awe that should characterize participation in the sacrament.

Churches that take communion seriously typically celebrate it more frequently, prepare their members more carefully, and approach it with greater reverence than churches that treat it as mere symbolism. This seriousness reflects the understanding that something real happens in the sacrament rather than just human remembrance of past events.

Embracing Spiritual Discipline

Churches could also benefit from embracing spiritual disciplines that develop spiritual strength and maturity. This might include regular fasting, structured prayer practices, spiritual direction, and other disciplines that have sustained Christian spirituality for centuries.

These disciplines don't constitute "works righteousness" but rather the means through which believers cooperate with God's grace in their spiritual development. Just as physical exercise develops physical strength, spiritual disciplines develop spiritual strength that enables believers to resist temptation, grow in holiness, and serve God more effectively.

Churches that incorporate spiritual disciplines into their regular practice typically produce more mature believers who are better equipped to handle life's challenges and more committed to Christian service. These disciplines provide the spiritual foundation that enables authentic Christian living rather than mere church attendance.

Recovering Liturgical Worship

Churches could also benefit from recovering liturgical worship that connects them to the broader Christian tradition and provides structure for meaningful encounter with God. This doesn't require adopting Catholic liturgy wholesale, but it does require moving beyond the entertainment-focused worship that characterizes many churches.

Liturgical worship provides a framework for corporate prayer, scripture reading, and sacramental celebration that has been refined over centuries of Christian practice. It connects local congregations to the universal church and provides continuity across cultures and generations.

Churches that embrace liturgical worship typically develop deeper spiritual roots and greater theological stability than churches that depend on contemporary music and motivational speaking for their spiritual impact. Liturgical worship focuses attention on God rather than on human performance and provides resources for spiritual growth that entertainment-focused worship cannot match.

CONCLUSION: THE PATH FORWARD

The abandonment of sacramental life represents one of the greatest losses in Christian history, but it's not irreversible. Churches and believers who recognize what was lost can work to recover the spiritual riches that were abandoned while maintaining the biblical insights that motivated the Reformation. It's good to remember that Martin Luther, the founder of the Reformation, still observed the sacraments and did not want them to be completely overturned and ignored.

This recovery requires acknowledging that the Catholic, Orthodx, Anglican, and many Lutheran denominations preserved important aspects of Christian tradition that modern churches need to rediscover. It doesn't require converting to Catholicism, but it does require humility about church limitations and openness to learning from Catholic wisdom.

The goal for Christians in our times should be to recover the spiritual depth and authenticity that characterized Christianity before it was reduced to entertainment, therapy, or social activism. This recovery requires embracing both the emphasis on biblical authority and the Catholic preservation of sacramental life and spiritual discipline.

Churches that successfully integrate these elements will provide their members with the spiritual resources necessary for authentic Christian living in a hostile culture. They will produce believers who are rooted in biblical truth, strengthened by sacramental grace, and disciplined through spiritual practice.

6

THE PURITY PRINCIPLE - WHY IGNORING SIN DESTROYS SOULS

THE MOST UNCOMFORTABLE TRUTH IN MODERN CHRISTIANITY IS THAT sexual purity matters to God. Yet this truth has become so foreign to contemporary American churches that most pastors avoid the subject entirely, leaving their congregations spiritually defenseless against the most destructive force in modern culture: the complete sexualization of human existence.

We live in a civilization drowning in sexual imagery, pornographic content, and hedonistic philosophy that treats sexual desire as the highest human good and sexual restraint as psychological damage. Every screen, every advertisement, every entertainment medium bombards believers with messages that directly contradict biblical teaching about sexuality, marriage, and human purpose. The result is a generation of Christians who know more about sexual techniques than sexual holiness, who can navigate dating apps but not biblical courtship, and who view pornography as normal while considering chastity as abnormal.

The silence of American churches on sexual purity represents one of the greatest pastoral failures in Christian history. While their congregations are being destroyed by sexual sin through pornography addiction, divorce, promiscuity, gender confusion, or the commodification of human sexuality, pastors preach about social justice, personal fulfillment, and positive thinking. They've abandoned their flocks to wolves while discussing the weather.

This abandonment has produced catastrophic results that extend far beyond individual moral failures to include the collapse of Christian marriage, the destruction of biblical gender roles, the acceptance of homosexual behavior, and the transformation of young women into narcissistic performers on platforms like Instagram and Only-Fans. The church's failure to teach and enforce sexual purity has contributed directly to the moral chaos that characterizes contemporary American culture.

Sexual purity isn't optional for Christians, it's a divine command that reflects God's design for human sexuality and his requirements for spiritual holiness. Understanding why purity matters, why it's so difficult to maintain, and why churches must address it directly is essential for any believer who wants to follow Christ faithfully in a hypersexualized culture.

The Biblical Foundation of Sexual Purity

Sexual purity is a biblical requirement that appears throughout Scripture as a fundamental aspect of Christian holiness. God's design for human sexuality is clear and non-negotiable: sexual expression belongs exclusively within the covenant of marriage between one man and one woman, and all other sexual activity constitutes sin that separates people from God.

God's Design for Sexuality

The biblical understanding of sexuality begins with God's creation of humans as male and female, designed for complementary relationship within the covenant of marriage. Genesis 2:24 establishes the pattern: "That is why a man leaves his father and mother and is united to his wife, and they become one flesh." This passage reveals that sexual union equates two people becoming one flesh in a way that reflects the unity between Christ and his church.

This design means that sexuality has sacred nature that extends far beyond personal gratification or emotional connection. Sexual union within marriage represents the deepest form of human intimacy, creating bonds that affect not just the couple but their children, their families, and their communities. When sexuality operates according to God's design, it produces blessings and spiritual growth. When it operates outside God's design, it produces spiritual death.

The New Testament reinforces this understanding through Paul's teaching about marriage as a picture of Christ's relationship with the church (Ephesians 5:31-32). This comparison reveals that sexual purity is about reflecting divine truth through human relationships. When believers maintain sexual purity, they demonstrate the faithfulness, commitment, and exclusive love that characterizes God's relationship with his people.

The Comprehensive Biblical Prohibition

Scripture consistently prohibits all sexual activity outside of marriage between one man and one woman. This prohibition isn't limited to adultery or prostitution but includes all forms of sexual immorality. This is where it becomes controversial to speak about the topics in modern contexts because it inherently includes fornication, homosexuality, pornography, and even lustful thoughts that treat other people as objects for sexual gratification.

Jesus established the standard for sexual purity in the Sermon on the Mount: "You have heard that it was said, 'You shall not commit adultery.' But I tell you that anyone who looks at a woman lustfully has already committed adultery with her in his heart" (Matthew 5:27-28). This teaching reveals that sexual purity involves not just external behavior but internal attitudes and desires.

Paul's teaching in 1 Corinthians 6:18-20 explains why sexual sin is uniquely destructive: "Flee from sexual immorality. All other sins a person commits are outside the body, but whoever sins sexually, sins against their own body. Do you not know that your bodies are temples of the Holy Spirit, who is in you, whom you have received from God? You are not your own; you were bought at a price. Therefore honor God with your bodies."

This passage solidifies sexual sin as a unique violation of the believer's relationship with God. Sexual immorality defiles the temple of the Holy Spirit and contradicts the believer's identity as someone purchased by Christ's blood. It represents a fundamental rejection of God's ownership and authority over human sexuality.

The comprehensive nature of biblical sexual ethics appears throughout the New Testament. Romans 1:24-27 condemns homosexual behavior as "shameful lusts" and "unnatural relations." 1 Corinthians 6:9-10 lists "the sexually immoral" and "men who have sex with men" among those who "will not inherit the kingdom of God." Galatians 5:19-21 includes "sexual immorality" and "debauchery" among the "acts of the flesh" that prevent people from inheriting God's kingdom.

These passages reflect God's unchanging design for human sexuality that applies to all people in all times. The consistency of biblical teaching on sexual purity demonstrates that this isn't a peripheral issue but a central aspect of Christian holiness.

The Positive Vision of Sexual Holiness

Biblical sexual ethics isn't primarily negative prohibition but positive vision of human sexuality operating according to divine design. The Song of Solomon celebrates sexual love within marriage as a beautiful reflection of God's passionate love for his people. Proverbs 5:18-19 encourages married men to "rejoice in the wife of your youth" and be "captivated by her love." Hebrews 13:4 declares that "marriage should be honored by all, and the marriage bed kept pure."

This positive vision reveals that sexual purity doesn't require the elimination of sexual desire but its proper channeling toward appropriate objects within appropriate relationships. God created sexual desire as a good gift that produces blessing when used according to his design and destruction when used contrary to his design.

The biblical vision of sexual holiness also includes the recognition that some people are called to celibacy - the complete renunciation of sexual activity for the sake of devotion to God's kingdom. Jesus himself lived as a celibate, and Paul recommended celibacy as a higher calling for those who could accept it (1 Corinthians 7:7-8). This calling demonstrates that sexual fulfillment isn't necessary for human happiness or spiritual maturity.

Whether expressed through faithful marriage or devoted celibacy, sexual holiness reflects the believer's commitment to honor God with their body and to demonstrate through their sexuality the faithfulness, purity, and exclusive devotion that characterizes God's relationship with his people.

The Modern Challenge of Hypersexualization

Contemporary American culture presents unprecedented challenges to sexual purity that previous generations of Christians never faced. The combination of technological innovation, cultural revolution, and moral collapse has created an environment where sexual temptation is constant, sexual restraint is mocked, and sexual purity is considered psychological damage rather than spiritual health.

The Pornography Epidemic

The most devastating assault on sexual purity comes from the pornography industry, which has transformed from a marginal vice into a mainstream entertainment medium that shapes sexual expectations and behaviors across all demographic groups. Internet pornography provides unlimited access to increasingly extreme sexual content that rewires the brain's reward systems and creates addictive patterns that destroy the capacity for healthy sexual relationships.

The statistics reveal the scope of this epidemic: over 90% of men and nearly 60% of women have been exposed to pornography, with the average age of first exposure now under 12 years old. Regular pornography use affects brain chemistry in ways similar to drug addiction, creating tolerance that requires increasingly extreme content to achieve the same stimulation. This progression often leads to sexual behaviors that would have been considered deviant just decades ago.

Pornography shapes cultural expectations about sexuality, relationships, and human worth. Young men develop unrealistic expectations about women's bodies and sexual performance. Young women feel pressure to conform to pornographic standards of beauty and behavior. Both sexes learn to view sexuality as performance rather than intimacy, consumption rather than covenant. While this often sounds like a feminist talking point, the reality is that constant exposure to this makes the desires become more explicit and extreme as time goes on, leading to all sorts of problems for the men who are broken by porn. It's the reason marginalized fetishes are now mainstream within society in a few short years of pornography being prevalent in our culture.

The church's failure to address pornography in recent times directly has left Christian families defenseless against this assault. Parents don't know how to protect their children from exposure or how to address addiction when it occurs. Married couples struggle with the impact of pornography on their relationships without pastoral guidance or church support. Single believers battle pornography addiction in isolation, often believing they're the only Christians struggling with this issue.

C.S. Lewis recognized the difficulty of sexual purity even before the internet age: "many people are deterred from seriously attempting Christian chastity because they think (before trying) that it is impossible. But when a thing has to be attempted, one must never think about possibility or impossibility. Faced with an optional question in an examination paper, one considers whether one can do it or not: faced with a compulsory question, one must do the best one can."

Lewis understood that sexual purity is a "compulsory question" for Christians, required by divine command regardless of difficulty. His insight becomes even more relevant in an age when pornography makes sexual temptation constant and sexual purity seemingly impossible.

The Social Media Narcissism Machine

Social media platforms have created new forms of sexual temptation and moral corruption that particularly target young women, transforming them into performers in a global attention economy that commodifies their sexuality and destroys their capacity for authentic relationships.

Instagram, TikTok, and similar platforms encourage young women to present themselves as sexual objects competing for male attention through increasingly revealing photos and provocative content. The platform algorithms reward this behavior with likes, comments, and followers, creating addictive feedback loops that drive users toward more extreme content.

This dynamic has produced a generation of young women who measure their worth by their ability to generate sexual attention from strangers online. They spend hours perfecting their appearance, crafting their online personas, and competing with other women for validation from men they'll never meet. The result is epidemic levels of anxiety, depression, and narcissistic personality traits among young women who should be developing authentic relationships and genuine self-worth.

The progression from Instagram attention-seeking to OnlyFans prostitution represents the logical endpoint of this commodification process. Young women who begin by posting revealing photos for free attention eventually discover they can monetize their sexuality through subscription-based pornography platforms. What begins as innocent social media use becomes literal prostitution facilitated by technology.

The church's failure to address social media's impact on young women has contributed directly to this moral catastrophe. Instead of teaching young women about biblical femininity, modesty, and authentic worth, churches have remained silent while their daughters are transformed into narcissistic performers competing in a sexual marketplace that destroys their capacity for marriage, motherhood, and spiritual growth.

The Normalization of Sexual Deviance

The hypersexualization of culture has led to the normalization of sexual behaviors that previous generations recognized as destructive and immoral. Divorce has become so common that many Christians view marriage as a temporary arrangement rather than a lifelong covenant. Cohabitation is accepted even in Christian circles as a normal step toward marriage. Homosexual behavior is celebrated as an alternative lifestyle rather than condemned as sexual sin.

This normalization occurs through a gradual process of cultural conditioning that makes abnormal behaviors seem normal through constant exposure and positive representation. When every television show includes divorced characters, every movie celebrates sexual promiscuity, and every news story presents homosexual relationships as equivalent to marriage, believers begin to question biblical teaching rather than cultural messaging.

The church's accommodation to this cultural pressure has accelerated the normalization process. Instead of maintaining biblical standards regardless of cultural opposition, many churches have modified their teaching to avoid offense or maintain cultural relevance. They've stopped preaching about sexual sin, stopped practicing church discipline for sexual immorality, and started affirming behaviors that Scripture clearly condemns.

This accommodation has produced generations of Christians who don't understand why sexual purity matters, don't know what biblical sexuality looks like, and don't have the spiritual resources necessary to resist cultural pressure toward sexual compromise. They've been left defenseless against the most powerful temptations of their time because their churches failed to equip them with biblical truth about sexuality.

The Devastating Consequences of Sexual Impurity

Beyond the simple scriptural commands regarding the topic, sexual sin produces practical consequences that destroy individuals, families, and entire cultures. Understanding these consequences is essential for appreciating why God prohibits sexual immorality and why churches must address this issue directly despite its difficulty and unpopularity.

The Destruction of Marriage and Family

Sexual impurity undermines the foundation of marriage by treating sexuality as individual gratification rather than covenant commitment. When people engage in sexual activity outside of marriage, they develop patterns of behavior and expectation that make faithful marriage difficult or impossible.

Pornography use, for example, creates unrealistic expectations about sexual performance and appearance that no real spouse can meet. Men who regularly consume pornography often struggle with sexual dysfunction in marriage because real intimacy cannot compete with the artificial stimulation of pornographic imagery. Women who compete for attention on social media often struggle to find satisfaction in the exclusive attention of one husband because they've become addicted to validation from multiple sources.

Premarital sexual activity creates similar problems by establishing patterns of sexual behavior divorced from commitment, sacrifice, and exclusive devotion. People who engage in casual sexual relationships learn to view sexuality as recreational activity rather than covenant expression, making the transition to faithful marriage psychologically and spiritually difficult.

The statistical evidence confirms these spiritual insights. Couples who cohabitate before marriage have significantly higher divorce rates than those who wait until marriage for sexual intimacy. Men who regularly use pornography report lower satisfaction with their marriages and higher rates of infidelity. Women who engage in promiscuous behavior before marriage struggle with depression, anxiety, and relationship instability throughout their lives.

These consequences aren't arbitrary punishments imposed by a harsh God - they're natural results of violating the design principles that God built into human sexuality. When sexuality operates outside its proper context, it produces destruction rather than blessing, chaos rather than order, death rather than life.

The Corruption of Children

Sexual impurity doesn't just affect adults but also corrupts children who are exposed to sexual content and behaviors before they have the maturity to process them properly. The early sexualization of children through pornography exposure, inappropriate media content, and adult sexual behavior creates trauma that affects their entire development.

Children who are exposed to pornography before puberty develop distorted understandings of sexuality that affect their capacity for healthy relationships throughout their lives. They learn to view sexuality as performance rather than intimacy, dominance rather than love, consumption rather than covenant. These distortions become deeply embedded in their psychological development and are extremely difficult to correct later in life.

The normalization of divorce teaches children that marriage is temporary and conditional rather than permanent and covenantal. Children from divorced homes have higher rates of relationship instability, sexual promiscuity, and emotional dysfunction throughout their lives. They struggle to trust others, commit to relationships, and believe in the possibility of lasting love.

The acceptance of homosexual behavior and gender confusion teaches children that biological sex is irrelevant and that sexual desire determines identity. This teaching produces epidemic levels of gender dysphoria, sexual confusion, and psychological instability among young people who should be developing secure identities based on biological reality and divine design.

The church's failure to protect children from sexual corruption represents one of the greatest pastoral failures in Christian history. Instead of creating environments where children can develop healthy understandings of sexuality, gender, and relationships, churches have allowed secular culture to shape their children's sexual development without biblical guidance or protection.

The Spiritual Consequences of Sexual Sin

Sexual immorality produces spiritual consequences that extend beyond psychological or relational damage to include separation from God, spiritual blindness, and eternal judgment. Paul's warning in 1 Corinthians 6:9-10 is clear: those who persist in sexual immorality "will not inherit the kingdom of God."

This warning isn't arbitrary divine preference but recognition that sexual sin contradicts the believer's relationship with God. Sexual immorality is rebellion against God's authority, rejection of his design for human sexuality, and preference for immediate gratification over eternal blessing.

Sexual sin also produces spiritual blindness that makes it difficult to perceive spiritual truth or respond to divine conviction. Romans 1:24-28 describes how God "gave them over" to sexual impurity as judgment for their rejection of his truth. This giving over isn't arbitrary punishment but natural consequence - people who persist in sexual sin lose their capacity to recognize spiritual reality.

The addictive nature of sexual sin makes it particularly destructive to spiritual growth. Unlike other sins that can be committed occasionally without creating dependency, sexual sin creates neurological patterns that demand regular satisfaction and increase in intensity over time. This addiction makes repentance difficult and spiritual growth nearly impossible without divine intervention and intensive accountability.

The church's failure to address sexual sin directly has left many believers trapped in patterns of behavior that prevent spiritual maturity and threaten eternal salvation. These believers may attend church regularly, participate in religious activities, and maintain Christian vocabulary while living in ways that contradict their profession of faith.

Pastoral Cowardice and Cultural Accommodation

Most pastors avoid preaching about sexual purity because they fear the negative response such messages would generate. They know that addressing pornography, premarital sex, divorce, or homosexuality will offend members, reduce attendance, and potentially cost them their positions. This fear reveals that these pastors serve their congregations rather than serving God, prioritizing human approval over divine command.

The cultural pressure to avoid "controversial" topics has intensified as American society has become increasingly hostile to biblical sexual ethics. Pastors who once felt comfortable preaching about sexual morality now face accusations of bigotry, hatred, and discrimination when they address these issues. The result is a generation of church leaders who have chosen cultural acceptance over biblical faithfulness.

This accommodation is a failure of pastoral courage and biblical authority. Pastors are called to be shepherds who protect their flocks from spiritual danger, not entertainers who avoid difficult topics to maintain popularity. When they refuse to address the sexual sins that are destroying their congregations, they abandon their most basic pastoral responsibility.

The Apostle Paul warned Timothy about this exact problem: "For the time will come when people will not put up with sound doctrine. Instead, to suit their own desires, they will gather around them a great number of teachers to say what their itching ears want to hear" (2 Timothy 4:3). American churches are filled with people who want to hear that their sexual behavior is acceptable to God, and they've found plenty of pastors willing to tell them what they want to hear.

The Therapeutic Gospel Replacement

Churches that avoid addressing sexual sin often replace biblical teaching with therapeutic messages that focus on emotional healing, self-acceptance, and personal fulfillment rather than repentance, holiness, and obedience to God's commands. This therapeutic approach treats sin as psychological dysfunction rather than moral rebellion against God. It may bring more people into Sunday services because it has a feel good message that's easy to digest in the morning, but this ignores a large part of what Christianity is about, abstaining from basic animal instincts and evils to become more in unison with God's will.

This replacement is particularly evident in how churches address issues like pornography addiction, sexual promiscuity, and gender confusion. Instead of calling these behaviors sin that requires repentance and transformation through God's grace, churches offer support groups, counseling services, and acceptance messages that validate people's struggles without calling them to biblical change.

The therapeutic gospel promises healing without holiness, acceptance without transformation, and comfort without conviction. It tells people that God loves them just as they are while ignoring God's call for them to become what he created them to be. This false gospel may make people feel better about themselves temporarily, but it cannot provide the spiritual transformation that actually solves their problems.

Biblical Christianity offers something far better than therapeutic comfort - it offers actual transformation through the power of the

Gospel. When churches abandon this transformative message in favor of therapeutic accommodation, they rob their congregations of the very power that can set them free from sexual bondage.

The Fear of Being "Judgmental"

The misinterpretation of Christ's teaching about judgment has created a generation of pastors who believe that identifying sin is itself sinful. They've been conditioned to think that calling sexual behavior sinful violates Christ's command to "judge not," leading them to avoid moral teaching entirely. I called out this passage before in this book, but the attempts to not judge anything has led Christians to spiral into meaninglessness in their faith which needs to be addressed again.

This misunderstanding ignores the clear biblical command for church leaders to "preach the word; be prepared in season and out of season; correct, rebuke and encourage—with great patience and careful instruction" (2 Timothy 4:2). Pastors cannot obey this command without identifying sin and calling for repentance, even when such messages are unpopular.

The fear of being judgmental has created churches where anything goes as long as people are sincere in their beliefs. Sexual immorality is tolerated, divorce is normalized, and even homosexual behavior is celebrated as long as it's expressed within "loving relationships." This tolerance isn't biblical love - it's pastoral negligence that allows people to continue in behaviors that will ultimately destroy them.

True biblical love requires truth-telling, even when that truth is difficult to hear. Pastors who refuse to address sexual sin aren't showing love to their congregations - they're showing cowardice that prioritizes their own comfort over their people's spiritual welfare.

THE DEVASTATING RESULTS OF PASTORAL SILENCE

The church's failure to address sexual sin has produced catastrophic results that extend far beyond individual moral failures to include the collapse of Christian marriage, the destruction of biblical gender roles, and the transformation of entire generations into sexual consumers rather than covenant partners.

The Normalization of Divorce

Churches that avoid teaching about sexual purity inevitably normalize divorce because they cannot address the sexual sins that destroy marriages. When pastors refuse to preach about pornography, adultery, or sexual selfishness, they leave married couples without the biblical resources necessary to build strong, lasting relationships.

The result is Christian divorce rates that match or exceed secular divorce rates, revealing that church attendance provides no protection against marital breakdown. Christian couples divorce for the same reasons as secular couples - sexual dissatisfaction, emotional disconnection, and the pursuit of personal happiness over covenant commitment - because their churches never taught them biblical alternatives.

Churches that do address divorce often focus on the symptoms rather than the causes, offering divorce recovery programs and remarriage ceremonies without addressing the sexual sins that destroyed the original marriages. This approach treats divorce as an unfortunate life event rather than the result of covenant breaking that requires repentance and restoration.

The normalization of divorce has created a generation of Christian children who view marriage as a temporary arrangement rather than a lifelong covenant. These children grow up expecting their own marriages to fail and lack the commitment necessary to work through the difficulties that all marriages face.

The Acceptance of Sexual Immorality

Churches that avoid preaching about sexual purity create environments where sexual immorality flourishes unchallenged. Congregation members engage in premarital sex, cohabitation, adultery, and pornography use without fear of church discipline or pastoral confrontation because these behaviors are never addressed from the pulpit.

This acceptance extends to church leadership, where pastors, elders, and staff members often struggle with the same sexual sins as their congregations without accountability or consequences. The result is spiritual leadership that lacks the moral authority necessary to address sexual issues because they're compromised by their own sexual failures.

The acceptance of sexual immorality also affects church programming and activities. Youth groups avoid teaching about sexual purity because it might make teenagers uncomfortable. Marriage ministries focus on communication skills rather than sexual holiness. Even premarital counseling often ignores sexual issues in favor of personality assessments and conflict resolution techniques.

This comprehensive avoidance creates churches where sexual sin is the elephant in the room that everyone knows about but no one discusses. Members struggle with sexual temptation and failure in isolation, believing they're the only Christians dealing with these issues because their churches never acknowledge that such problems exist.

The Rise of Sexual Confusion

The church's silence on sexual issues has created a vacuum that secular culture has filled with messages that directly contradict biblical teaching. Young people who receive no sexual instruction from their churches learn about sexuality from pornography, social media, and popular culture that promote values completely opposed to Christian teaching.

This cultural indoctrination has produced epidemic levels of sexual confusion among Christian young people who don't understand God's design for sexuality, gender, or relationships. They struggle with gender dysphoria, sexual identity questions, and relationship dysfunction because their churches failed to provide biblical foundation for understanding these fundamental aspects of human existence.

The rise of LGBTQ+ ideology in Christian circles directly results from this pastoral failure. When churches don't teach biblical sexuality, their members become vulnerable to secular ideologies that promise to answer the questions their churches avoided. Young people who never learned that God created them male and female for complementary relationships become easy targets for ideologies that promise alternative identities and relationships.

Churches that finally attempt to address these issues often discover that their members have already been thoroughly indoctrinated by secular sexual ideology and are resistant to biblical teaching. The window for providing foundational sexual education has closed, and these churches must now engage in remedial teaching that attempts to undo years of cultural conditioning.

THE BIBLICAL MANDATE FOR SEXUAL TEACHING

Scripture provides clear mandates for church leaders to address sexual issues directly and comprehensively, making the modern church's silence a direct violation of biblical commands rather than a matter of pastoral discretion or cultural sensitivity.

The Apostolic Example

The apostles regularly addressed sexual issues in their letters to early churches, demonstrating that sexual teaching is essential rather than optional for church leadership. Paul's letters contain extensive instruction about sexual morality, marriage relationships, and the consequences of sexual sin.

In 1 Corinthians 5, Paul addresses a case of sexual immorality within the church and commands the congregation to remove the offending member until he repents. This passage demonstrates that churches must not only teach about sexual purity but also enforce sexual standards through church discipline when necessary.

Paul's teaching in 1 Corinthians 6:18-20 explains why sexual sin requires special attention: "Flee from sexual immorality. All other sins a person commits are outside the body, but whoever sins sexually, sins against their own body. Do you not know that your bodies are temples of the Holy Spirit, who is in you, whom you have received from God? You are not your own; you were bought at a price. Therefore honor God with your bodies."

This passage reveals that sexual sin is uniquely destructive because it violates the believer's body, which is the temple of the Holy Spirit.

Churches that ignore sexual sin allow their members to defile the very temples where God dwells, making pastoral silence on sexual issues a form of sacrilege.

The Comprehensive Biblical Sexual Ethic

Scripture provides comprehensive teaching about sexual morality that covers every aspect of human sexuality from singleness to marriage to widowhood. This teaching isn't limited to a few isolated verses but permeates both the Old and New Testaments as a fundamental aspect of God's design for human relationships.

The biblical sexual ethic begins with God's creation of humans as male and female, designed for complementary relationship within the covenant of marriage (Genesis 1:27, 2:24). This design establishes marriage between one man and one woman as the only appropriate context for sexual expression, making all other sexual activity sinful.

The New Testament reinforces this ethic through extensive teaching about sexual purity, marriage relationships, and the consequences of sexual immorality. Romans 1:24-27 condemns homosexual behavior as "shameful lusts" and "unnatural relations." 1 Corinthians 6:9-10 lists various forms of sexual immorality among the sins that prevent people from inheriting God's kingdom. Hebrews 13:4 commands that "marriage should be honored by all, and the marriage bed kept pure."

This comprehensive biblical teaching makes it impossible for faithful pastors to avoid sexual issues while claiming to preach the whole counsel of God. Churches that ignore sexual morality are ignoring substantial portions of Scripture and failing to equip their members with the biblical knowledge necessary for holy living.

The Pastoral Responsibility

Scripture places specific responsibility on church leaders to address sexual issues as part of their pastoral calling. Pastors are commanded to "preach the word" (2 Timothy 4:2), which includes the biblical teaching about sexual morality. They're called to "shepherd the flock of God" (1 Peter 5:2), which includes protecting the flock from sexual predators and sexual sin.

The qualifications for church elders include being "the husband of one wife" and managing their households well (1 Timothy 3:2, 4), demonstrating that sexual integrity is essential for church leadership. Leaders who lack sexual integrity cannot provide the moral authority necessary to address sexual issues in their congregations.

Pastors are also responsible for church discipline, which includes addressing sexual immorality when it occurs within the congregation. Matthew 18:15-17 provides the process for confronting sin within the church, and 1 Corinthians 5 demonstrates that sexual sin requires church discipline when the offender refuses to repent.

Churches that avoid addressing sexual sin are violating these clear biblical mandates and failing in their most basic pastoral responsibilities. They're allowing their members to continue in behaviors that will ultimately destroy them while claiming to love and serve them.

THE PATH TO RECOVERY

Churches that want to recover their biblical mandate to address sexual sin must overcome the cultural pressure, pastoral cowardice, and theological confusion that have created the current crisis. This recovery requires courage, commitment, and a willingness to prioritize biblical truth over cultural acceptance.

Pastoral Courage and Biblical Authority

The first step in recovery requires pastors who are willing to preach biblical truth about sexual morality regardless of the cultural consequences. These pastors must understand that their authority comes from God rather than from their congregations and that their primary responsibility is faithfulness to Scripture rather than popularity with people.

This courage must be grounded in deep conviction about the authority of Scripture and the necessity of sexual purity for spiritual health. Pastors who are uncertain about biblical teaching on sexual issues or who doubt the relevance of biblical sexual ethics for contemporary life will lack the conviction necessary to address these issues effectively.

Pastoral courage also requires personal integrity in sexual matters.

Pastors who struggle with pornography, marital unfaithfulness, or other sexual sins cannot provide the moral authority necessary to address these issues in their congregations. They must first address their own sexual failures before they can help others achieve sexual purity.

Churches must also support pastors who demonstrate this courage by standing with them when they face criticism for biblical teaching about sexual morality. Congregations that demand biblical preaching must be willing to defend their pastors when such preaching generates controversy or opposition.

Comprehensive Sexual Education

Churches that want to address sexual sin effectively must provide comprehensive biblical education about sexuality, marriage, and relationships. This education must provide age-appropriate instruction that builds biblical understanding of God's design for human sexuality.

This education must address the specific sexual challenges that contemporary believers face, including pornography addiction, social media temptation, dating relationships, and marriage preparation. It cannot rely on generic moral teaching but must provide practical guidance for living sexually pure lives in a hypersexualized culture.

Churches must also provide resources for sexual healing and restoration for those who have been damaged by sexual sin. This includes counseling services, support groups, and accountability relationships that help people overcome sexual addiction and develop healthy patterns of sexual behavior.

The goal of this education isn't merely behavioral modification but spiritual transformation that addresses the heart of the issues underlying sexual sin. Churches must help people understand that sexual purity flows from love for God and desire for holiness rather than from fear of consequences or social pressure.

Church Discipline and Restoration

Churches that take sexual sin seriously must be willing to practice church discipline when members persist in sexual immorality despite pastoral instruction and personal confrontation. This discipline isn't punishment but restoration - an attempt to bring wayward members back to fellowship with God and the church.

Church discipline must follow the biblical pattern outlined in Matthew 18:15-17, beginning with private confrontation and escalating to public discipline only when private efforts fail. The goal is always restoration rather than condemnation, and discipline should be accompanied by offers of help, counseling, and support for those who are willing to repent.

Churches must also be prepared to welcome back those who repent of sexual sin and demonstrate genuine change in their behavior. The goal of discipline is restoration, and churches that practice discipline without offering restoration have missed the point of the biblical process.

This balance between discipline and restoration requires wisdom, compassion, and commitment to both truth and grace. Churches that emphasize discipline without grace become legalistic and harsh. Churches that emphasize grace without discipline become permissive and ineffective.

The church's failure to address sexual sin represents one of the greatest pastoral failures in American Christianity, but it's not irreversible. Churches that are willing to recover their biblical mandate to teach sexual purity, practice church discipline, and provide comprehensive sexual education can still make a difference in the lives of their members and their communities.

The alternative is continued spiritual devastation as sexual sin destroys marriages, corrupts children, and undermines the church's witness to the world. The choice is clear: churches can continue their cowardly silence and watch their congregations be destroyed by sexual sin, or they can find the courage to speak biblical truth about sexuality and provide their members with the resources necessary for sexual purity and spiritual health.

7

WHAT MODERN CHRISTIANS CAN
LEARN FROM ORTHODOXY

THE MOST SURPRISING RELIGIOUS TREND IN AMERICA TODAY IT'S THE conversion of young people to Catholicism or Orthodox churches. While Churchian institutions hemorrhage members and struggle to attract anyone under forty, the Catholic Church is experiencing what the National Catholic Register calls a "conversion boom," with some dioceses reporting 30% to 70% increases in new converts, most of them young adults fleeing the spiritual wasteland of modern American Christianity.

Sydney Johnston, a thirty-year-old Columbia graduate, spent two years visiting dozens of denominations before converting to Catholicism. Her explanation reveals why so many young people are making the same choice: "There's just something so beautiful and transcendent about the rituals and the ancient history in the Catholic Mass that's been preserved. The church really communicates a degree of reverence that I didn't find in the more liberal, laissez-faire approach of nondenominational churches."

Adrian Lawson, a software developer from Southern California, discovered Catholicism through online debates about church history. His conclusion after extensive research: "I had anxiety, depression, and panic attacks, but since I've started praying the rosary regularly, I haven't had any of those issues." As a catechist at his parish, he estimates a 50% year-over-year increase in converts, noting that they tend to be "more traditional" and "a little more fervent and a little more forceful in their beliefs."

These conversions represent more than individual spiritual journeys but also the bankruptcy of attempts to remain culturally relevant through entertainment, casual worship, and theological flexibility. Young people can get entertainment anywhere. They don't need churches to provide concert-quality music, motivational speaking, or social media-friendly experiences. What they can't get anywhere else is authentic encounter with the transcendent God who calls his people to be separate from the world.

The Catholic and Orthodox Churches offer what many churches have abandoned: historical continuity, sacramental depth, theological stability, and the recognition that Christianity is supposed to be different from secular culture rather than indistinguishable from it. While modern churches chase cultural trends and modify their message to avoid offense, the Catholic Church maintains the same liturgy, the same sacraments, and the same teachings that have sustained Christians for two millennia.

This isn't necessarily an argument for converting to Catholicism, though many readers may reach that conclusion on their own. This is an argument for understanding what Christianity lost in its rush to be relevant and what it must recover if it wants to survive the spiritual crisis that threatens to destroy American Christianity entirely. The idea of returning to tradition is a positive one and can be seen in many protestant churches stemming from more traditional Lutheran denominations and Anglican churches as well. The core message is we must reject modernism in all of its forms.

The Biblical Vision of Church Unity

Christ's prayer for his followers in John 17:20-23 reveals God's intention for church unity: "My prayer is not for them alone. I pray also for those who will believe in me through their message, that all of them may be one, Father, just as you are in me and I am in you. May they also be in us so that the world may believe that you have sent me.

I have given them the glory that you gave me, that they may be one as we are one - I in them and you in me - so that they may be brought to complete unity. Then the world will know that you sent me and have loved them even as you have loved me."

This prayer describes organic unity that reflects the unity between the Father and the Son. Christ prayed for his followers to be one in the same way that he and the Father are one, creating a unity so profound that it would convince the world of his divine mission.

Paul's description of the church as Christ's body reinforces this vision of organic unity: "Just as a body, though one, has many parts, but all its many parts form one body, so it is with Christ. For we were all baptized by one Spirit so as to form one body - whether Jews or Gentiles, slave or free - and we were all given the one Spirit to drink" (1 Corinthians 12:12-13).

The body metaphor reveals that church unity is essential to the church's nature and function. Body parts cannot survive when separated from the whole, and individual Christians cannot thrive when separated from the unified body of Christ. The thousands of denominations represent a dismembered body rather than a healthy organism. This unity has to stem from something, and tradition and orthodoxy are matters that Christians can all join in together to bring about said unity of the body.

Ephesians 4:4-6 emphasizes the theological foundation of church unity: "There is one body and one Spirit, just as you were called to one hope when you were called; one Lord, one faith, one baptism; one God and Father of all, who is over all and through all and in all." This passage describes seven "ones" that should produce visible unity among believers rather than the fragmentation that characterizes modern Christianity.

The Catholic Claim to Apostolic Unity

The Catholic Church claims to be the one, holy, catholic, and apostolic church that Christ established, maintaining unbroken continuity with the apostles through apostolic succession and preserving the unity that Christ prayed for through submission to papal authority and adherence to apostolic tradition.

This claim is based on historical evidence and theological necessity. The Catholic Church can trace its leadership back to Peter and the apostles through an unbroken chain of episcopal ordination. Its liturgy preserves elements that date to the apostolic period. Its core doctrines were established by the same councils that determined the biblical canon.

More importantly, the Catholic Church has maintained visible unity across cultures, languages, and centuries in ways that denominations have never achieved. A Catholic Mass in Nigeria follows the same basic structure as a Mass in Ireland or Mexico. Catholic doctrine remains consistent whether taught in Rome or rural America. Catholic moral teaching doesn't change based on cultural pressure or popular opinion.

What's interesting is the Catholic Church has more diversity in thought than many are taught in modern America. This includes multiple rites, various theological schools, and different spiritual traditions. But this diversity exists within unity rather than creating division. Catholics can disagree about theological opinions, pastoral strategies, and political issues while maintaining communion with the same church, submission to the same authority, and participation in the same sacraments.

Churchian attempts to achieve unity through ecumenical dialogue or denominational cooperation have failed because they lack the theological foundation and institutional structure necessary for genuine unity. Without apostolic succession, magisterial authority, and sacramental communion, churches remain voluntary associations that can cooperate but cannot unite.

The Scandal of Division

The division of Christianity into thousands of competing denominations represents one of the greatest scandals in Christian history. These divisions contradict Christ's prayer for unity, undermine the church's witness to the world, and create confusion about Christian truth that drives people away from faith entirely.

The multiplication of denominations follows a predictable pattern: theological disagreement leads to institutional separation, which leads to the formation of new denominations that eventually experience their own theological disagreements and institutional separations. This process has produced not just major denominational families but thousands of independent churches that recognize no authority beyond their own interpretation of Scripture.

This fragmentation makes it impossible for churches to speak with unified voice on moral issues, theological questions, or cultural challenges. When denominations disagree about fundamental issues like the nature of salvation, the authority of Scripture, or the definition of marriage, they cannot provide clear guidance to believers or credible witness to unbelievers.

The scandal becomes even greater when churches divide over secondary issues like worship styles, church governance, or pastoral personalities. These divisions suggest that unity is so fragile that it cannot survive disagreements about matters that have nothing to do with essential Christian doctrine.

Young people recognize this fragmentation as evidence of Christianity's instability and inauthenticity. They see churches splitting over trivial issues, denominations changing their positions based on cultural pressure, and pastors starting new churches whenever they disagree with existing leadership. This instability makes Christianity appear to be a human institution rather than a divine establishment.

THE AUTHORITY OF SACRED TRADITION

The Catholic and Orthodox Churches' preservation of sacred tradition provides theological stability and historical continuity that churches lack. While modern churches base their authority solely on Scripture interpreted by individual believers or denominational leaders, the Catholic and Orthodox Churches recognize both Scripture and tradition as sources of divine revelation that work together to preserve apostolic truth.

The Biblical Foundation of Tradition

Modern churches claim to follow "Scripture alone," but this principle isn't found in Scripture itself. Instead, the Bible consistently emphasizes the importance of oral tradition alongside written revelation. Paul's instruction to Timothy reveals the proper relationship between Scripture and tradition: "But as for you, continue in what you have learned and have become convinced of, because you know those from whom you learned it, and how from infancy you have known the Holy Scriptures, which are able to make you wise for salvation through faith in Christ Jesus" (2 Timothy 3:14-15).

This passage shows that Timothy learned Christian truth from both the Holy Scriptures and from the people who taught him - the oral tradition that preserved apostolic teaching alongside written revelation. Paul doesn't present Scripture and tradition as competing authorities but as complementary sources of divine truth.

Paul's instruction to the Thessalonians makes this even clearer: "So then, brothers and sisters, stand firm and hold fast to the teachings we passed on to you, whether by word of mouth or by letter" (2 Thessalonians 2:15). This verse explicitly commands believers to maintain both written teachings (Scripture) and oral teachings (tradition) that the apostles delivered.

The early church operated according to this principle for centuries before the biblical canon was finalized. Christians preserved apostolic teaching through oral tradition, liturgical practice, and ecclesiastical authority while the New Testament was being written, collected, and recognized as Scripture. The same church that preserved tradition also determined which books belonged in the biblical canon.

The Development of Doctrine

The Catholic understanding of tradition doesn't mean that new doctrines can be invented or that church teaching can contradict Scripture. Instead, tradition represents the organic development of apostolic truth as the church gains deeper understanding of divine revelation through the guidance of the Holy Spirit.

This development follows the principle that Christ established in John 16:12-13: "I have much more to say to you, more than you can now bear. But when he, the Spirit of truth, comes, he will guide you into all the truth. He will not speak on his own; he will speak only what he hears, and he will tell you what is yet to come."

This promise indicates that the apostles didn't receive complete understanding of Christian truth all at once but would be guided into fuller understanding over time. The development of doctrine represents the fulfillment of this promise as the church, under the guidance of the Holy Spirit, comes to understand more fully the implications of apostolic revelation.

The doctrine of the Trinity provides the clearest example of this development. The word "Trinity" doesn't appear in Scripture, and the full theological understanding of the Trinity wasn't articulated until the fourth century. But this doctrine represents the church's deeper understanding of biblical revelation about the Father, Son, and Holy Spirit rather than the invention of new truth.

These churches that reject the authority of tradition often end up rejecting doctrines that depend on traditional development. Some groups have rejected the Trinity, the dual nature of Christ, or the authority of the biblical canon because these doctrines cannot be proven from Scripture alone without reference to traditional interpretation.

The Magisterium and Doctrinal Stability

The Catholic Church's teaching authority, called the Magisterium, provides doctrinal stability that churches cannot achieve through individual interpretation of Scripture. The Magisterium consists of the Pope and bishops in communion with him, who possess the authority to interpret Scripture and tradition authoritatively for the entire church.

This authority doesn't mean that the Pope or bishops can invent new doctrines or contradict Scripture. Instead, the Magisterium serves as the guardian and interpreter of the deposit of faith that was delivered to the apostles. Its role is to preserve apostolic truth, clarify disputed questions, and protect the church from doctrinal error.

The promise of Christ in Matthew 16:18-19 provides the foundation for this authority: "And I tell you that you are Peter, and on this rock I will build my church, and the gates of Hades will not overcome it. I will give you the keys of the kingdom of heaven; whatever you bind on earth will be bound in heaven, and whatever you loose on earth will be loosed in heaven."

This promise indicates that Christ established institutional authority within the church that would preserve it from fundamental error. The "gates of Hades" represent the forces of evil and error that constantly assault the church, but Christ promised that these forces would not overcome the church he built on Peter.

The practical result of magisterial authority is doctrinal stability that has preserved Catholic teaching for two millennia. While denominations change their positions on fundamental issues like the authority of Scripture, the nature of salvation, or the definition of marriage, Catholic doctrine remains consistent across centuries and cultures.

This stability doesn't mean that Catholic teaching never develops or that pastoral practices never change. But it does mean that core doctrines remain stable while their implications are explored more fully and their applications are adapted to new circumstances.

THE LITURGICAL CONNECTION TO HEAVEN

The Catholic Mass provides a foretaste of heavenly worship that connects earthly believers with the eternal liturgy described in the book of Revelation. This connection isn't metaphorical or symbolic - it's sacramental reality that makes the Mass a participation in heavenly worship rather than merely a human religious activity.

The Heavenly Liturgy in Revelation

The book of Revelation describes heavenly worship in terms that correspond directly to the structure and elements of the Catholic Mass. Revelation 4:8-11 presents the basic pattern: "Each of the four living creatures had six wings and was covered with eyes all around, even under its wings. Day and night they never stop saying: 'Holy, holy, holy is the Lord God Almighty, who was, and is, and is to come.' Whenever the living creatures give glory, honor and thanks to him who sits on the throne and who lives for ever and ever, the ten elders fall down before him who sits on the throne and worship him who lives for ever and ever. They lay their crowns before the throne and say: 'You are worthy, our Lord and God, to receive glory and honor and power, for you created all things, and by your will they were created and have their being.'"

This heavenly worship includes the "Holy, holy, holy" that forms the Sanctus in the Catholic Mass, the prostration and adoration that characterizes Catholic liturgy, and the recognition of God's worthiness that pervades Catholic prayer. The correspondence isn't accidental - the Mass participates in the same worship that occurs eternally in heaven.

Revelation 5:6-14 describes the worship of the Lamb who was slain, corresponding to the Eucharistic sacrifice that forms the center of the Mass. The heavenly liturgy focuses on the sacrificial death of Christ, just as the Mass makes present the same sacrifice that Christ offered on Calvary. The "new song" that the heavenly creatures sing corresponds to the liturgical music that accompanies the Mass.

Revelation 7:9-17 describes the multitude from every nation worshiping before the throne, corresponding to the universal character of Catholic worship that unites believers across cultures and languages in the same liturgical action. The "white robes" that the saints wear correspond to the liturgical vestments that symbolize the purity required for divine worship.

The Mass as Heavenly Participation

The Catholic understanding of the Mass isn't that it represents or symbolizes heavenly worship but that it actually participates in the eternal liturgy that occurs in heaven. When Catholics attend Mass, they join the angels and saints in the worship that never ceases before the throne of God.

This participation occurs through the sacramental principle that physical actions can convey spiritual realities. The bread and wine become the actual body and blood of Christ, making his sacrifice present on the altar. The prayers and songs unite with the heavenly liturgy. The congregation joins the communion of saints in worshiping the triune God.

The Second Vatican Council's Constitution on the Sacred Liturgy explains this participation: "In the earthly liturgy we take part in a foretaste of that heavenly liturgy which is celebrated in the holy city of Jerusalem toward which we journey as pilgrims, where Christ is sitting at the right hand of God, a minister of the holies and of the true tabernacle."

This understanding transforms the Mass from a human religious activity into a divine encounter that transcends time and space. Catholics participate in the eternal reality of his priesthood and the ongoing offering of his sacrifice in heaven.

As mentioned earlier in the chapter, Orthodox Churches, Anglican, and many Lutheran denominations follow many of these same traditions similar to the mass that millions of Christians partake in apart from it. While this is certainly written from a pro-Catholic perspective, not every church has abandoned these sacred traditions and moving toward tradition is the goal to keep in mind here.

The Contrast with Modern Worship

Modern worship services, no matter how well-intentioned or emotionally moving, cannot provide this connection to heavenly worship because they lack the sacramental structure that makes such participation possible. Without the real presence of Christ in the Eucharist, without apostolic succession that connects earthly clergy to heavenly priesthood, and without liturgical tradition that preserves the forms of heavenly worship, services remain human activities rather than divine encounters.

This doesn't mean that God cannot work through worship or that believers cannot experience genuine spiritual blessing in their services. But it does mean that worship lacks the objective sacramental reality that makes Catholic worship a participation in heavenly liturgy rather than merely a human expression of religious devotion.

The entertainment-focused worship that characterizes many churches actually moves in the opposite direction from heavenly worship. Instead of lifting believers into the transcendent realm of divine worship, it brings worship down to the level of human entertainment and emotional manipulation.

Young people recognize this difference intuitively. They can get better entertainment at concerts, better motivation from self-help speakers, and better social connection from clubs and organizations. What they cannot get anywhere else is authentic encounter with the transcendent God who calls them out of the world and into his eternal kingdom.

THE AUTHENTICITY THAT ATTRACTS YOUNG PEOPLE

The conversion of young people to Catholicism and Orthodoxy reveals their hunger for authenticity in a culture saturated with artificial experiences, manufactured emotions, and marketing manipulation. churches that have tried to attract young people through contemporary music, casual worship, and culturally relevant messaging have discovered that these strategies backfire because they feel inauthentic, and they are inauthentic.

Young people can get better entertainment at concerts, better motivation from TED talks, and better social experiences at clubs and organizations. When churches try to compete with secular entertainment, they inevitably lose because they're playing a game they were never meant to play.

The Failure of "Relevant" Christianity

The Churchian obsession with cultural relevance has produced churches that look and sound exactly like the secular culture they're trying to reach. These churches use the same music styles, the same communication techniques, and the same marketing strategies as secular organizations, making them indistinguishable from the world they claim to be separate from.

This approach fundamentally misunderstands what young people are actually seeking. They're not looking for churches that mirror their secular experiences - they're looking for something different, something transcendent, something that connects them to realities beyond the material world they encounter everywhere else.

Christ himself warned against this worldly approach: "If you belonged to the world, it would love you as its own. As it is, you do not belong to the world, but I have chosen you out of the world. That is why the world hates you" (John 15:19). Churches that try to make the world love them by becoming like the world have abandoned their calling to be separate and distinct.

The "relevant" Christianity that churches have embraced actually makes Christianity irrelevant by eliminating the very qualities that make it unique and valuable. When churches sound like motivational seminars, look like entertainment venues, and feel like social clubs, they offer nothing that young people cannot find elsewhere in more polished and professional forms.

The Appeal of Ancient Tradition

Young people converting to Catholicism and Orthodoxy consistently cite the appeal of ancient tradition, historical continuity, and connection to something larger than themselves. They're drawn to liturgy that has been refined over centuries, prayers that connect them to believers across history, and practices that have sustained Christians through persecution, plague, and cultural upheaval.

This appeal reveals a deep hunger for rootedness in a culture characterized by constant change, technological disruption, and social fragmentation. Young people who have grown up with social media, consumer culture, and political polarization are seeking stability, depth, and meaning that transcends contemporary trends.

The Catholic Mass provides this stability through its unchanging structure, ancient prayers, and sacramental focus. Whether celebrated in a cathedral or a simple parish church, whether attended by hundreds or dozens, the Mass maintains the same essential character that has defined Catholic worship for centuries.

Modern churches that change their worship styles every few years to stay current cannot provide this stability. Their constant adaptation to cultural trends signals that they lack confidence in their own traditions and are more concerned with popularity than with faithfulness to their calling.

The Hunger for Transcendence

Young people are also drawn to traditional worship because it provides genuine encounter with transcendence rather than manufactured emotional experiences. The traditional understanding of the Mass as participation in heavenly worship creates an atmosphere of reverence and awe that contemporary worship often lacks.

This transcendence flows from the sacramental reality of Christ's presence in the Eucharist and the liturgical structure that has been designed to facilitate encounter with the divine. Young people recognize this authenticity and respond to it even when they don't fully understand the theology behind it.

Modern churches that have abandoned transcendent worship in favor of entertainment-focused services have eliminated the very element that makes worship distinctive from secular experiences. When worship becomes primarily about human emotion and entertainment, it loses its power to connect believers with the eternal realities that give meaning to temporal existence.

The hunger for transcendence also explains why young people are drawn to traditional Catholic practices like Eucharistic adoration, the rosary, and liturgical prayer. These practices provide structured ways of encountering God that don't depend on emotional manipulation or contemporary relevance for their effectiveness.

The Rejection of Consumer Christianity

Young people often explicitly reject the consumer mentality that characterizes much of Christianity. They're tired of being treated like customers whose preferences must be accommodated and whose satisfaction must be maintained through constant innovation and entertainment.

The Catholic and Orthodox Churches' refusal to modify their core teachings and practices based on popular opinion appeals to young people who are seeking truth rather than validation. They want to be challenged, transformed, and called to something higher than their current spiritual condition rather than being told that they're fine just as they are.

This rejection of consumer Christianity also extends to the prosperity gospel and therapeutic Christianity that have infected many churches. Young people recognize these approaches as spiritual junk food that provides temporary satisfaction while failing to address their deeper spiritual needs.

The emphasis on sacrifice, discipline, and spiritual growth through suffering appeals to young people who have been raised on messages of self-esteem and personal fulfillment but have discovered that these messages don't provide lasting satisfaction or meaning.

THE CHURCHIAN RESPONSE: DOUBLING DOWN ON FAILURE

Rather than learning from the Catholic and Orthodox Churches' success in attracting young converts, many churches have responded by doubling down on the very strategies that are driving young people away. They've become even more entertainment-focused, even more culturally accommodating, and even more consumer-oriented in their desperate attempts to remain relevant.

The Megachurch Model's Bankruptcy

The megachurch model that has dominated Churchianity for decades is increasingly recognized as spiritually bankrupt by young people who are seeking authentic Christian community rather than religious entertainment. These massive operations may attract crowds, but they cannot provide the personal relationships, spiritual depth, and authentic worship that young people are seeking.

Megachurches operate more like corporations than churches, with professional staff, marketing departments, and customer service approaches that treat congregants like consumers rather than disciples. This corporate model may be efficient for managing large numbers of people, but it cannot provide the spiritual intimacy and personal accountability that characterize authentic Christian community.

Young people who have grown up in megachurch environments often report feeling spiritually empty despite years of church attendance. They've been entertained, motivated, and inspired, but they haven't been transformed, challenged, or connected to the transcendent realities that give life meaning.

The megachurch model's emphasis on numerical growth over spiritual depth has produced churches that are miles wide but inches deep, attracting crowds while failing to make disciples. Young people recognize this shallowness and are seeking alternatives that provide genuine spiritual substance.

The Worship Wars' Irrelevance

Modern churches continue to fight "worship wars" over musical styles, liturgical formats, and generational preferences while missing the deeper issues that actually matter to young people. These debates about contemporary versus traditional music, formal versus casual dress, and modern versus ancient liturgy focus on surface issues while ignoring the spiritual emptiness that characterizes much worship.

Young people converting to Catholicism aren't primarily motivated by musical preferences or liturgical styles - they're motivated by the search for authentic encounter with God. They're willing to embrace unfamiliar musical forms and ancient liturgical practices if these provide genuine spiritual substance.

The obsession with worship styles reveals a fundamental misunderstanding of what worship is supposed to accomplish. Worship isn't primarily about human preference or cultural relevance - it's about encountering the living God in ways that transform human hearts and minds.

Churches that focus on making worship appealing to contemporary tastes often end up making it appealing to no one because they eliminate the very elements that make worship distinctive and powerful. Young people can get better music at concerts and better entertainment at theaters - what they cannot get elsewhere is authentic worship of the transcendent God.

The Seeker-Sensitive Failure

The seeker-sensitive movement that has influenced churches for decades has failed to produce the spiritual growth and evangelistic success that it promised. Churches that have modified their worship, watered down their teaching, and eliminated potentially offensive elements have discovered that these changes don't actually attract seekers or produce mature believers.

Young people are particularly resistant to seeker-sensitive approaches because they recognize them as marketing strategies rather than authentic spiritual practices. They want to be challenged and transformed rather than accommodated and entertained.

The seeker-sensitive model also assumes that non-Christians are primarily interested in comfort and familiarity when they visit churches. But many young seekers are actually looking for something different from their secular experiences - something that challenges their assumptions, expands their understanding, and connects them to transcendent realities.

The Catholic Church's refusal to modify its worship and teaching to accommodate seeker preferences actually makes it more attractive to serious seekers who are looking for authentic spiritual truth rather than religious entertainment.

Doctrinal Stability in a Changing World

Young people are drawn to doctrinal stability in a world characterized by constant change and moral relativism. While denominations modify their positions on fundamental issues like biblical authority, sexual morality, and the nature of salvation, the Catholic Church maintains consistent teaching across centuries and cultures.

This stability provides young people with a solid foundation for their beliefs and values in a culture that offers few fixed reference points. They don't have to worry that their church will change its position on fundamental issues based on cultural pressure or popular opinion.

The Catholic Church's doctrinal stability also provides intellectual satisfaction for young people who are seeking coherent worldviews that can withstand philosophical scrutiny. Catholic theology has been developed and refined over two millennia, creating a comprehensive system that addresses fundamental questions about God, humanity, and the meaning of existence.

Modern churches that constantly modify their teaching to accommodate contemporary sensibilities cannot provide this intellectual stability. Their theological flexibility may seem appealing in the short term, but it ultimately undermines confidence in their authority and reliability.

The Universal Church Experience

Young people are also attracted to the experience of participating in the same liturgy, receiving the same sacraments, and sharing the same faith with believers around the world. This universality provides a sense of connection to the global Christian community that denominationalism cannot match.

When young Catholics travel, they can attend Mass anywhere in the world and participate in worship that follows the same basic structure and includes the same essential elements. This universality creates a sense of belonging to something larger than local congregations or national churches.

Modern churches, with their thousands of denominations and independent congregations, cannot provide this universal experience. Young Churchians who travel often discover that churches in different locations have completely different worship styles, theological emphases, and cultural characteristics.

The Catholic Church's universality also extends across time, connecting contemporary believers with the saints and martyrs who have maintained the same faith throughout history. This historical continuity provides young people with a sense of participating in something eternal rather than temporary.

The Challenge of Discipleship

Perhaps most importantly, the Catholic and Orthodox churches attract young people because they take discipleship seriously rather than trying to make Christianity easy or comfortable. Catholic and Orthodox teaching about sacrifice, suffering, and spiritual discipline appeals to young people who are seeking meaning and purpose rather than entertainment and comfort.

The emphasis on saints and martyrs provides young people with examples of radical Christian commitment that inspire them to pursue spiritual excellence rather than spiritual mediocrity. These examples demonstrate that Christianity is supposed to be challenging, transformative, and costly rather than easy, comfortable, and convenient.

Modern churches that have eliminated the challenging aspects of Christianity in their attempts to attract crowds have actually made Christianity less attractive to serious seekers. Young people who are looking for meaning and purpose in their lives are not satisfied with a Christianity that demands nothing and promises everything.

The conversion of young people to Catholicism represents more than individual spiritual journeys - it reveals the bankruptcy of attempts to remain culturally relevant through entertainment, accommodation, and consumer-focused ministry. Young people are rejecting these approaches because they recognize them as inauthentic substitutes for genuine spiritual encounter.

Modern churches that want to attract and retain young people must learn from the Catholic Church's success by emphasizing substance over style, truth over relevance, and transformation over entertainment. They must recover the transcendent worship, doctrinal stability, and spiritual challenge that make Christianity distinctive from secular alternatives.

The alternative is continued decline as young people seek elsewhere for the authentic spiritual experiences that their churches have abandoned in their pursuit of cultural relevance. The choice is clear: churches can continue chasing cultural trends while losing their spiritual substance, or they can recover the ancient faith that has sustained Christians for two millennia and continues to attract those who are serious about following Christ.

8

THE GENERATIONAL CURSE - HOW BAD THEOLOGY DESTROYS FAMILIES

ONE OF THE MOST DESTRUCTIVE HERESIES INFILTRATING AMERICAN churches today masquerades as biblical teaching about "generational sin" or "generational curses." This false doctrine, popularized by prosperity preachers and social justice advocates alike, teaches that the sins of previous generations automatically transfer to their descendants, creating inherited guilt that requires special spiritual intervention to break.

This heresy has found its most sophisticated expression in the preaching of Tony Evans, whose YouTube sermon "Stop the Cycle of Generational Sin" has been viewed millions of times and adopted by countless pastors who use it to justify everything from racial guilt manipulation to prosperity gospel fundraising schemes. Evans' teaching represents a masterclass in biblical misinterpretation that takes Scripture out of context, ignores clear theological principles, and produces practical results that contradict the Gospel itself.

The generational sin doctrine has become particularly popular among churches promoting social justice ideology because it provides theological justification for collective racial guilt. White Christians are told they bear responsibility for slavery, segregation, and systemic racism because these sins have been passed down through generations, creating spiritual curses that can only be broken through confession, reparations, and submission to social justice demands.

This teaching contradicts the clear biblical teaching about individual responsibility, undermines the sufficiency of Christ's atonement, and creates false guilt that drives believers away from the Gospel's message of complete forgiveness through faith in Jesus Christ.

Understanding why the generational sin doctrine is heretical requires examining its biblical foundations, theological implications, and practical consequences. Only then can Christians recognize this deception and return to the biblical teaching about sin, forgiveness, and spiritual inheritance that actually transforms lives and builds healthy families.

THE BIBLICAL TEACHING ON INDIVIDUAL RESPONSIBILITY

The foundation of biblical theology regarding sin and guilt is individual responsibility before God. While sin certainly has consequences that affect families and communities, the Bible consistently teaches that each person bears responsibility only for their own sins and cannot inherit guilt from previous generations.

Ezekiel's Clear Refutation

The most direct biblical refutation of generational sin doctrine appears in Ezekiel 18, where God explicitly rejects the idea that children bear guilt for their parents' sins. The chapter begins with God addressing a popular proverb that sounds remarkably similar to modern generational sin teaching: "The word of the Lord came to me: 'What do you mean by repeating this proverb concerning the land of Israel, "The parents have eaten sour grapes, and the children's teeth are set on edge"?'" (Ezekiel 18:1-2).

This proverb expressed the same idea that Tony Evans and other generational sin teachers promote, that the actions of previous generations create consequences that their descendants must bear. The Israelites were using this proverb to explain their current suffering as the result of their ancestors' sins rather than taking responsibility for their own spiritual condition.

God's response is unambiguous: "As surely as I live, declares the Sovereign Lord, you will no longer quote this proverb in Israel. For everyone belongs to me, the parent as well as the child - both alike belong to me. The one who sins is the one who will die" (Ezekiel 18:3-4).

This declaration establishes the principle of individual responsibility that governs all of God's dealings with humanity. Each person belongs to God individually, each person is responsible for their own choices, and each person bears the consequences of their own sins rather than inheriting guilt from their ancestors.

God reinforces this principle throughout the chapter with specific examples: "Suppose there is a righteous man who does what is just and right... He will surely live, declares the Sovereign Lord. But suppose this son has a violent son, who sheds blood or does any of these other things... Will such a man live? He will not! Because he has done all these detestable things, he is to be put to death; his blood will be on his own head" (Ezekiel 18:5, 9-13).

The passage continues with the opposite scenario: "But suppose this son has a son who sees all the sins his father commits, and though he sees them, he does not do such things... He will not die for his father's sin; he will surely live" (Ezekiel 18:14, 17).

These examples demonstrate that righteousness and wickedness are individual choices that produce individual consequences. A righteous father cannot save a wicked son through his righteousness, and a wicked father cannot damn a righteous son through his wickedness. Each person stands before God based on their own choices rather than their family history.

Deuteronomy's Confirmation

Deuteronomy 24:16 provides additional confirmation of individual responsibility: "Parents are not to be put to death for their children, nor children put to death for their parents; each will die for their own sin." This command established the principle of individual justice in Israel's legal system, preventing the punishment of innocent family members for crimes they didn't commit.

This principle reflects God's character and his standards for human justice. If human courts cannot justly punish children for their parents' crimes, how much more does divine justice require individual responsibility rather than inherited guilt?

The historical books demonstrate this principle in practice. When King Amaziah executed the officials who had murdered his father, "he did not put the children of the assassins to death, in accordance with what is written in the Book of the Law of Moses where the Lord commanded: 'Parents shall not be put to death for their children, nor children put to death for their parents; each will die for their own sin'" (2 Kings 14:6).

This example shows that even in cases of the most serious crimes the principle of individual responsibility prevented punishment of the criminals' children. If human justice requires individual responsibility in such extreme cases, divine justice certainly cannot operate on principles of inherited guilt.

The New Testament Confirmation

The New Testament reinforces the principle of individual responsibility through its teaching about salvation, judgment, and spiritual accountability. Romans 14:12 states clearly: "So then, each of us will give an account of ourselves to God." This verse makes individual accountability the basis of divine judgment rather than family history or generational patterns.

Paul's teaching about salvation emphasizes individual faith rather than family heritage: "Yet to all who did receive him, to those who believed in his name, he gave the right to become children of God - children born not of natural descent, nor of human decision or a husband's will, but born of God" (John 1:12-13). Spiritual birth depends on individual faith rather than natural descent or family spiritual condition.

Christ emphasized individual responsibility in his teaching about judgment: "But I tell you that everyone will have to give account on the day of judgment for every empty word they have spoken. For by your words you will be acquitted, and by your words you will be condemned" (Matthew 12:36-37). Each person will be judged based on their own words and actions rather than their family's spiritual history.

The parable of the talents (Matthew 25:14-30) illustrates individual accountability in spiritual matters. Each servant received different amounts and was judged based on his individual stewardship rather than his family background or the performance of other servants. The faithful servants were rewarded individually, and the unfaithful servant was punished individually.

TONY EVANS' THEOLOGICAL ERRORS

Tony Evans' sermon "Stop the Cycle of Generational Sin" represents a sophisticated attempt to defend generational sin doctrine through biblical interpretation, but his arguments collapse under careful examination. Evans makes several fundamental theological errors that reveal his misunderstanding of Scripture and his accommodation to social justice ideology.

Misinterpreting Exodus 20:5

Evans' primary biblical support comes from Exodus 20:5, which states: "You shall not bow down to them or worship them; for I, the Lord your God, am a jealous God, punishing the children for the sin of the parents to the third and fourth generation of those who hate me." Evans interprets this verse as establishing a principle of inherited guilt that passes automatically from parents to children.

This interpretation ignores the context and conditions of the passage. The verse specifically addresses idolatry, defined as"bowing down" and "worshiping" false gods, rather than establishing a general principle about all sin. More importantly, the punishment applies to "those who hate me," indicating that the children must also choose to hate God and practice idolatry to experience the consequences.

The passage describes the natural consequences of idolatrous families rather than arbitrary punishment of innocent children. When parents worship false gods, they typically raise their children to do the same, creating patterns of rebellion that produce judgment. But the children experience consequences because they choose to continue their parents' idolatry, not because they inherit guilt automatically.

Deuteronomy 7:9-10 clarifies this principle: "Know therefore that the Lord your God is God; he is the faithful God, keeping his covenant of love to a thousand generations of those who love him and keep his commandments. But those who hate him he will repay to their face by destruction; he will not be slow to repay to their face those who hate him."

This passage shows that both blessings and curses depend on individual choice - loving God and keeping his commandments versus hating him and rejecting his commands. The consequences extend to multiple generations because children typically follow their parents' spiritual choices, not because guilt transfers automatically.

Confusing Consequences with Curses

Evans consistently confuses the natural consequences of sin with supernatural curses that require special spiritual intervention to break. He describes patterns of behavior - alcoholism, divorce, abuse, poverty - as "generational curses" that bind families until they're broken through prayer, confession, and spiritual warfare.

This confusion creates several theological problems. First, it treats natural consequences as supernatural phenomena, leading believers to seek spiritual solutions for problems that may require practical intervention. Second, it suggests that Christ's atonement is insufficient to deal with certain types of sin, requiring additional spiritual work to achieve complete freedom.

The biblical understanding of sin's consequences is much simpler. Sin produces natural results that affect individuals, families, and communities. These consequences can create patterns that influence future generations, but they don't create supernatural curses that require special spiritual intervention beyond the normal means of grace.

For example, alcoholism often runs in families because children learn drinking patterns from their parents, inherit genetic predispositions to addiction, and grow up in environments where alcohol abuse is normalized. These factors create strong influences toward alcoholism, but they don't create supernatural curses that can only be broken through spiritual warfare.

The solution to such patterns involves both spiritual and practical elements: repentance from sin, faith in Christ's forgiveness, renewal of the mind through Scripture, accountability relationships, and often professional help for addiction recovery. But it doesn't require special prayers to "break generational curses" or elaborate spiritual warfare techniques.

Undermining the Sufficiency of Christ's Atonement

Evans' teaching about generational curses ultimately undermines the sufficiency of Christ's atonement by suggesting that some sins require additional spiritual work beyond simple faith in Christ's finished work. If generational curses can only be broken through special prayers, confession of ancestral sins, or spiritual warfare techniques, then Christ's death on the cross was insufficient to deal with all sin.

This theological error contradicts the clear biblical teaching about the completeness of Christ's atonement. Colossians 2:13-14 declares: "When you were dead in your sins and in the uncircumcision of your flesh, God made you alive with Christ. He forgave us all our sins, having canceled the charge of our legal indebtedness, which stood against us and condemned us; he has taken it away, nailing it to the cross."

The phrase "all our sins" includes any sins that might be considered "generational." Christ's atonement doesn't leave any category of sin unaddressed or require additional spiritual work to achieve complete forgiveness. When believers place their faith in Christ, they receive complete forgiveness for all sin - past, present, future, individual, and any supposed "generational" guilt.

Galatians 3:13 reinforces this truth: "Christ redeemed us from the curse of the law by becoming a curse for us, for it is written: 'Cursed is everyone who is hung on a pole.'" If Christ redeemed believers from "the curse of the law" - the ultimate curse that separated humanity from God - then no lesser "generational curses" can remain in effect for those who are in Christ.

The generational curse doctrine essentially teaches that Christ's atonement was incomplete, that some sins require additional spiritual work, and that believers can remain under curses despite being redeemed by Christ's blood. This teaching contradicts the Gospel itself and robs believers of the assurance that comes from understanding the completeness of Christ's work.

THE SOCIAL JUSTICE APPLICATION

The generational sin doctrine has found its most destructive application in social justice ideology, where it's used to justify collective racial guilt and demand reparations for historical injustices. Churches promoting this application teach that white Americans bear responsibility for slavery, segregation, and systemic racism because these sins have been passed down through generations, creating spiritual curses that affect entire racial groups.

The Racial Guilt Manipulation

Social justice advocates use generational sin doctrine to argue that white Christians must confess and repent for sins they never committed, pay reparations for injustices they never perpetrated, and submit to social justice demands to break the "generational curses" of racism and white supremacy.

This application reveals the political rather than pastoral motivation behind much generational sin teaching. Instead of helping individuals deal with personal sin and family dysfunction, it's used to advance political agendas and redistribute wealth based on racial categories.

The racial application of generational sin doctrine creates several logical and theological problems. First, it assumes that racial categories are spiritually significant in ways that contradict biblical teaching about unity in Christ. Galatians 3:28 declares: "There is neither Jew nor Gentile, neither slave nor free, nor is there male and female, for you are all one in Christ Jesus."

This verse doesn't eliminate racial distinctions or cultural differences, but it does eliminate their spiritual significance for believers. Christians are united by their common identity in Christ rather than divided by their racial heritage. The generational sin doctrine that focuses on racial guilt contradicts this fundamental Gospel truth.

Second, the racial application ignores the historical reality that many white Americans have no ancestral connection to slavery or segregation. Millions of white Americans descended from immigrants who arrived after slavery was abolished, from families who opposed slavery, or from ethnic groups that experienced their own persecution and discrimination.

The generational sin doctrine would make these Americans guilty of sins their ancestors never committed, in places their families never lived, against people their families never encountered. This application reveals the arbitrary and unjust nature of collective guilt based on racial categories.

The Biblical Response to Racism

My letter of admonishment to my church leadership addressed this issue directly by pointing out that the modern concept of racism, as commonly defined by social justice advocates, is not actually a sin according to biblical standards. The Bible consistently recognizes ethnic and cultural distinctions while calling believers to love and justice toward all people.

Christ demonstrated proper ethnic recognition in his encounter with the Canaanite woman (Matthew 15:21-28). When she asked him to heal her daughter, he initially refused, saying, "I was sent only to the lost sheep of Israel" and "It is not right to take the children's bread and toss it to the dogs."

According to modern definitions of racism, Christ's response would be considered racist because he prioritized his own ethnic group and used language that could be considered derogatory toward Gentiles. But Scripture presents this as an example of proper mission priorities and ethnic awareness rather than sinful racism.

Since Christ cannot sin by his nature, maintaining community solidarity with one's ethnic group and making judgments based on cultural differences cannot be inherently sinful. The Bible consistently shows God working through ethnic distinctions rather than eliminating them, choosing specific peoples for specific purposes while maintaining love and justice toward all.

The Apostle Peter's vision in Acts 10 didn't eliminate ethnic distinctions but revealed that the Gospel was intended for all ethnic groups. The Jerusalem Council in Acts 15 didn't condemn ethnic awareness but determined how Jewish and Gentile believers could maintain their cultural distinctives while sharing fellowship in Christ.

The biblical response to ethnic tensions isn't the elimination of all distinctions or the confession of collective guilt, but the recognition that all people are created in God's image, all people are sinners in need of salvation, and all people can be reconciled to God and each other through faith in Jesus Christ.

THE PROSPERITY GOSPEL CONNECTION

The generational curse doctrine has found fertile ground in prosperity gospel theology, where it's used to explain why some believers don't experience the health and wealth that prosperity preachers promise. When followers don't receive the blessings they've been taught to expect, prosperity teachers blame "generational curses" that prevent God's blessings from manifesting.

The Fundraising Scheme

Prosperity preachers use generational curse teaching to generate revenue through "curse-breaking" services, special offerings to "break generational poverty," and products designed to help believers identify and eliminate generational hindrances to their prosperity.

This application reveals the mercenary motivation behind much generational curse teaching. Instead of helping believers understand biblical truth about sin and forgiveness, it's used to extract money from vulnerable people who are desperate for solutions to their problems.

The prosperity gospel version of generational curses typically focuses on financial issues - "generational poverty," "family patterns of lack," or "ancestral agreements with poverty spirits." Believers are taught that their financial struggles result from curses that can only be broken through special prayers, seed offerings, or spiritual warfare techniques.

This teaching creates tremendous guilt and confusion among believers who struggle financially despite their faith in Christ. Instead of understanding that financial difficulties are normal aspects of life in a fallen world, they're taught that their problems indicate spiritual failure or unbroken generational curses.

The False Promise of Breakthrough

The generational curse doctrine promises "breakthrough" from family patterns and inherited limitations through spiritual techniques that go beyond simple faith in Christ. This promise appeals to people who are frustrated with ongoing struggles and looking for spiritual solutions to practical problems.

But the promised breakthrough rarely materializes because the doctrine is based on false premises. Financial problems usually result from economic conditions, poor decisions, lack of education, or other practical factors rather than supernatural curses. Relationship problems typically stem from poor communication skills, unresolved conflicts, or incompatible personalities rather than generational patterns that require spiritual warfare to break.

When the promised breakthrough doesn't occur, believers are told they haven't prayed hard enough, haven't identified all the generational curses, or haven't given enough money to support the ministry. This creates a cycle of spiritual manipulation that keeps believers trapped in false hope while enriching the teachers who promote these doctrines.

The biblical promise of transformation through Christ is both more realistic and more powerful than the false promises of generational curse teaching. Scripture promises that believers are "new creations" in Christ (2 Corinthians 5:17), but this transformation occurs through the normal means of grace - Scripture reading, prayer, fellowship, and obedience to God's commands - rather than through special spiritual techniques.

Creating False Guilt in Parents

Parents who embrace generational curse teaching often develop paralyzing guilt about the impact their sins might have on their children. Instead of understanding that their children are responsible for their own choices, these parents believe that every mistake they make creates spiritual curses that will damage their children for generations.

This false guilt prevents parents from exercising proper authority and discipline because they fear creating additional "generational patterns" that their children will inherit. They become paralyzed by the fear that their imperfections will doom their children to repeat their mistakes.

The biblical understanding of parental responsibility is both more realistic and more hopeful. Parents are called to train their children in God's ways (Deuteronomy 6:4-9), provide discipline and instruction (Proverbs 22:6), and model godly living (1 Corinthians 11:1). But they cannot guarantee their children's spiritual outcomes because each child must make individual choices about following God.

This understanding frees parents to do their best while trusting God with the results. They can acknowledge their imperfections, seek forgiveness when they fail, and continue training their children without the crushing weight of believing that their mistakes will create generational curses.

Undermining Generational Blessing

The focus on generational curses often overshadows the biblical teaching about generational blessing that God intends to flow from faithful parents to their children. Psalm 112:1-2 declares: "Praise the Lord. Blessed are those who fear the Lord, who find great delight in his commands. Their children will be mighty in the land; the generation of the upright will be blessed."

This passage describes the positive inheritance that godly parents can leave their children - not automatic salvation or guaranteed success, but the blessing that comes from growing up in homes where God is honored and his commands are followed.

Proverbs 13:22 reinforces this principle: "A good person leaves an inheritance for their children's children, but a sinner's wealth is stored up for the righteous." The inheritance described here includes both material and spiritual blessings that flow from righteous living.

The generational curse doctrine discourages parents from recognizing and celebrating these positive inheritances. Instead of focusing on the blessings they can pass to their children through faithful living, parents become obsessed with identifying and breaking supposed curses from previous generations.

Preventing Healthy Tradition

The generational curse teaching often leads believers to reject all family traditions, cultural practices, and ancestral connections as potentially cursed or spiritually dangerous. This rejection prevents the healthy transmission of wisdom, values, and positive traditions that strengthen families and communities.

The Bible presents a balanced view of generational inheritance that includes both positive and negative elements. Children naturally learn from their parents' examples, inherit their parents' strengths and weaknesses, and grow up in environments shaped by their parents' choices. This inheritance includes both blessings and challenges, but it doesn't include automatic guilt or supernatural curses.

Wise parents acknowledge the negative patterns in their family history while working to break them through godly living and biblical training. They also celebrate and preserve the positive traditions, values, and practices that have strengthened their families across generations.

The generational curse doctrine prevents this balanced approach by treating all family patterns as potentially cursed and requiring spiritual intervention to break. This approach destroys family identity, cultural heritage, and the natural bonds that connect generations together.

THE TRUE BIBLICAL TEACHING ON GENERATIONAL INFLUENCE

The Bible does recognize that parents' choices affect their children and that family patterns can influence multiple generations. But this influence operates through natural consequences and learned behaviors rather than supernatural curses that require special spiritual intervention to break.

Natural Consequences and Learned Behaviors

When parents make sinful choices, their children often experience the natural consequences of those choices and learn patterns of behavior that they may repeat in their own lives. This process doesn't involve supernatural curse transmission but natural cause and effect relationships that operate according to God's design for family life.

For example, children of alcoholic parents often struggle with addiction themselves because they inherit genetic predispositions, learn dysfunctional coping mechanisms, and grow up in environments where alcohol abuse is normalized. These factors create strong influences toward addiction, but they don't create supernatural curses that can only be broken through spiritual warfare.

Similarly, children from divorced homes often struggle with relationship stability because they lack models of successful marriage, develop trust issues from their parents' failed relationship, and learn patterns of conflict resolution that damage their own marriages. These influences are powerful and real, but they operate through natural psychological and social processes rather than supernatural curse mechanisms.

The Power of Godly Example

The positive side of generational influence appears when parents model godly living and create environments where children learn biblical values and behaviors. This positive influence doesn't guarantee that children will follow their parents' example, but it provides them with the knowledge, skills, and motivation necessary for godly living.

Timothy provides the biblical example of positive generational influence. Paul writes: "I am reminded of your sincere faith, which first lived in your grandmother Lois and in your mother Eunice and, I am persuaded, now lives in you also" (2 Timothy 1:5).

This passage describes the transmission of faith across three generations from grandmother to mother to son. But this transmission occurred through teaching, example, and influence rather than automatic spiritual inheritance. Timothy had to choose to embrace the faith that his grandmother and mother modeled for him.

The biblical pattern for breaking negative generational patterns is simple: repent of sin, place faith in Christ, renew the mind through Scripture, and begin modeling godly behavior for the next generation. This process doesn't require special prayers to break generational curses or elaborate spiritual warfare techniques - it requires the normal Christian life lived faithfully over time.

CONCLUSION: RETURNING TO BIBLICAL TRUTH

The generational curse doctrine represents one of the most destructive heresies affecting American churches today because it undermines fundamental Gospel truths while appearing to offer spiritual solutions to real problems. This false teaching contradicts the biblical principles of individual responsibility, the sufficiency of Christ's atonement, and the nature of spiritual inheritance.

Churches that embrace this doctrine inevitably drift toward either prosperity gospel manipulation or social justice ideology because the underlying theology supports both applications. The focus on breaking generational curses leads naturally to fundraising schemes that promise spiritual breakthrough through financial giving or political activism that demands collective confession and reparations for historical injustices.

The solution isn't more sophisticated curse-breaking techniques or better methods for identifying generational patterns - it's returning to the simple biblical truth that each person is responsible for their own choices, Christ's atonement is sufficient for all sin, and spiritual transformation occurs through the normal means of grace rather than special spiritual techniques.

Parents who want to break negative family patterns should focus on their own spiritual growth, biblical parenting practices, and godly example rather than elaborate prayers to break generational curses. Churches that want to help families should teach biblical truth about sin, forgiveness, and sanctification rather than promoting false doctrines that create guilt and confusion.

The Gospel itself provides the only solution to generational problems: "Therefore, if anyone is in Christ, the new creation has come: The old has gone, the new is here!" (2 Corinthians 5:17). This promise doesn't require additional spiritual work to break generational curses - it requires simple faith in the finished work of Jesus Christ.

When believers understand that they are new creations in Christ, freed from all condemnation and guilt, they can address family problems with confidence rather than fear, hope rather than despair, and practical wisdom rather than spiritual manipulation. They can acknowledge the influence of their family history while taking responsibility for their own choices and trusting God to transform their lives through his grace.

The generational curse doctrine promises more than it can deliver while undermining the very Gospel truths that actually transform lives and families. Churches that abandon this false teaching and return to biblical truth about individual responsibility and Christ's sufficient atonement will find that the Gospel itself provides all the power necessary to break negative patterns and build godly families that honor God across generations.

9

THE REMNANT - FINDING AND BUILDING FAITHFUL CHURCHES

THE SPIRITUAL WASTELAND OF AMERICAN CHURCHIANITY HAS LEFT millions of believers searching for authentic Christian community that prioritizes biblical truth over cultural accommodation, spiritual transformation over entertainment, and eternal significance over temporal comfort. For those who recognize the corruption we've documented throughout this book, the question becomes urgent: Where can faithful Christians find churches that actually follow Christ rather than following the world?

The answer isn't simple because the cancer of compromise has spread so thoroughly through denominations that finding untainted congregations requires careful discernment and often difficult choices. But faithful churches do exist - scattered remnants that have maintained biblical authority, sacramental depth, and spiritual discipline despite the cultural pressure to conform to worldly standards.

The search for authentic Christianity has led many believers to an unexpected destination: the Catholic Church as stated before. The current Jubilee Year 2025, with its theme "Pilgrims of Hope," provides a perfect opportunity for believers to examine what they've lost and consider what the Catholic Church has preserved through two millennia of faithful witness.

This isn't necessarily an argument for converting to Catholicism, though many readers may reach that conclusion after honest examination of the evidence. This is an argument for understanding what authentic Christianity looks like and where it can be found in an age when most churches have abandoned their divine mission for worldly success.

THE JUBILEE YEAR OPPORTUNITY

The Catholic Church's celebration of Jubilee Year 2025 offers believers a unique opportunity to experience authentic Christian worship, teaching, and community that has been preserved through centuries of cultural change and persecution. The Jubilee theme "Pilgrims of Hope" speaks directly to believers who have become spiritual refugees from churches that no longer provide the spiritual nourishment they desperately need.

The Biblical Foundation of Jubilee

The concept of Jubilee originates in Leviticus 25:8-55, where God commanded the Israelites to celebrate a year of Jubilee every fifty years as "a time to rest the land and its agricultural workers, release slaves, and return land to its original owners." The key passage declares: "Proclaim liberty throughout all the land to all its inhabitants. It shall be a jubilee for you" (Leviticus 25:10).

This biblical foundation reveals that Jubilee represents liberation, restoration, and renewal - exactly what believers need after decades of spiritual captivity to false gospels, entertainment Christianity, and cultural accommodation. The Jubilee offers freedom from the spiritual slavery that characterizes much of American Churchianity.

Isaiah 61:1-2 connects the Jubilee to the Messiah's mission: "The Spirit of the Lord God is upon me... to proclaim the year of the Lord's favor." Christ himself applied this prophecy to his ministry in Luke 4:18-19, linking the Jubilee to his mission of salvation and spiritual liberation. The Catholic Church's celebration of Jubilee Year continues this mission of spiritual liberation for those trapped in false forms of Christianity.

The Catholic Jubilee Tradition

The Catholic Church has celebrated Jubilee years for over seven centuries, traditionally occurring every twenty-five years as times of "special grace, forgiveness, and renewal." These celebrations offer opportunities for pilgrimage, indulgences, and spiritual growth that provide exactly what believers have been missing in their entertainment-focused churches.

Pope Francis called Jubilee 2025 to "celebrate hope and invite Catholics worldwide to deepen their faith." But this invitation extends beyond Catholics to include all Christians who are seeking authentic spiritual renewal. The Jubilee also celebrates "the 1,700th anniversary of the First Council of Nicaea," connecting contemporary believers to the fundamental Christian truth "that Jesus is both true God and true man" - a teaching that many churches have abandoned in their rush to be culturally relevant.

The Pope's message for the Jubilee captures what refugees are seeking: "May the light of Christian hope illumine every man and woman, as a message of God's love addressed to all!" This hope isn't the false hope of prosperity gospel promises or therapeutic Christianity's self-help messages - it's the authentic hope of eternal salvation through Jesus Christ.

Pilgrimage as Spiritual Journey

The Jubilee emphasis on pilgrimage provides a perfect metaphor for believers who have become spiritual pilgrims searching for authentic Christian community. The traditional Jubilee practices - "visiting designated holy sites, such as the four major basilicas in Rome or local churches in dioceses" - symbolize "a journey of faith and conversion" that many believers desperately need.

This pilgrimage isn't just physical travel but spiritual journey from false Christianity to authentic faith, from entertainment to worship, from consumer religion to sacramental life. Believers who participate in Jubilee activities often discover what they've been missing in their own churches: reverent worship, sacramental grace, and connection to the historical Christian tradition.

The Jubilee also offers "special indulgences, which are remissions of the temporal punishment of already forgiven sins." While modern theology has traditionally rejected indulgences, the underlying principle - that spiritual practices can provide grace and blessing beyond ordinary means - appeals to believers who have been starved of sacramental life in their modern churches.

IDENTIFYING FAITHFUL CHURCHES

For believers who aren't ready to consider Catholicism, the challenge becomes identifying churches that have maintained biblical faithfulness despite the cultural pressure to compromise. This identification requires careful evaluation of doctrine, practice, and spiritual fruit rather than relying on denominational labels or popular reputation.

Essential Doctrinal Standards

Faithful churches must maintain unwavering commitment to biblical authority as the final standard for faith and practice. This means rejecting the cultural accommodation that has led many churches to modify their teaching on sexual morality, gender roles, and other controversial issues. Churches that change their positions based on cultural pressure have demonstrated that they serve culture rather than Christ.

The doctrine of salvation must remain centered on justification by faith alone through grace alone, without the additions of works righteousness or the subtractions of cheap grace that eliminate the necessity of repentance and transformation. Churches that preach either legalistic works-salvation or antinomian license have abandoned the biblical Gospel.

The authority of Scripture must be maintained without compromise, rejecting both liberal higher criticism that undermines biblical reliability and fundamentalist literalism that ignores proper hermeneutical principles. Churches must preach the whole counsel of God, including the difficult passages that contemporary culture finds offensive.

The nature of Christ as fully God and fully man must be affirmed without compromise, rejecting both ancient heresies and modern attempts to reduce Christ to a moral teacher or social activist. Churches that present Christ primarily as an example to follow rather than as Savior to trust have abandoned essential Christian doctrine.

Liturgical and Sacramental Depth

Faithful churches should demonstrate reverence for worship that reflects the holiness of God rather than the entertainment preferences of contemporary culture. This doesn't require specific liturgical forms, but it does require worship that focuses on God rather than on human emotion or entertainment.

The sacraments of baptism and communion should be treated as means of grace rather than mere symbols, celebrated with appropriate frequency and reverence. Churches that rarely celebrate communion or treat it as an afterthought have lost sight of its central importance in Christian worship.

Church discipline should be practiced according to biblical standards, addressing serious sin within the congregation while maintaining the goal of restoration rather than condemnation. Churches that avoid discipline entirely have abandoned their responsibility to maintain holiness within the Christian community.

Preaching should be expository rather than topical, working through entire books of Scripture rather than cherry-picking verses that support predetermined themes. Faithful churches should address the full range of biblical teaching, including the difficult passages that contemporary culture finds offensive.

Spiritual Fruit and Community Life

Faithful churches should produce spiritual fruit in the lives of their members rather than just providing religious entertainment or social services. This fruit includes growth in holiness, commitment to biblical values, and sacrificial service to others rather than self-centered pursuit of personal fulfillment.

The church community should be characterized by genuine relationships based on shared commitment to Christ rather than social compatibility or demographic similarity. Members should demonstrate love for one another that transcends cultural, economic, and racial divisions.

Church leadership should demonstrate personal holiness and biblical knowledge rather than just charismatic personality or professional competence. Pastors should be able to teach Scripture accurately, provide spiritual counsel, and model Christian living for their congregations.

The church's mission should focus on making disciples rather than attracting crowds, measuring success by spiritual transformation rather than numerical growth or financial prosperity. Churches that prioritize attendance numbers over spiritual depth have adopted worldly rather than biblical standards of success.

THE CATHOLIC ALTERNATIVE RECONSIDERED

For believers who have honestly evaluated their options and found faithful churches lacking, the Catholic Church presents an alternative that deserves serious consideration. The Catholic Church has preserved elements of authentic Christianity that most churches have abandoned, offering spiritual resources that believers desperately need.

Historical Continuity and Apostolic Succession

The Catholic Church's claim to apostolic succession provides historical continuity that churches cannot match. While denominations trace their origins to various reformers and revival movements, the Catholic Church traces its leadership directly to Peter and the apostles through an unbroken chain of episcopal ordination.

This continuity provides theological stability and spiritual authority that churches lack. Catholic doctrine has remained consistent across centuries and cultures because it's grounded in apostolic tradition rather than individual interpretation or cultural accommodation.

The Catholic Church's preservation of ancient liturgical forms connects contemporary believers to the worship practices of early Christians in ways that contemporary worship cannot. When Catholics participate in the Mass, they join a liturgical tradition that extends back to the apostolic period.

This historical continuity provides spiritual rootedness that appeals to believers who have grown tired of the constant innovation and cultural accommodation that characterizes modern churches. They find stability in traditions that have sustained Christians through persecution, plague, and cultural upheaval.

Sacramental Life and Spiritual Discipline

The Catholic Church's preservation of the seven sacraments provides comprehensive spiritual resources that address every stage and challenge of Christian life. From baptism to confirmation to marriage to anointing of the sick, the sacraments offer divine grace through physical means that honor both the spiritual and material aspects of human existence.

This sacramental system creates a rhythm of grace that structures the entire Christian life around encounters with God rather than around entertainment or social activities. Catholic believers have regular opportunities to receive forgiveness through confession, spiritual nourishment through the Eucharist, and divine blessing through the other sacraments.

The Catholic Church has also preserved spiritual disciplines - fasting, prayer, meditation, pilgrimage - that develop spiritual strength and maturity. These disciplines aren't optional extras for super-spiritual Catholics but normal aspects of Catholic life that help believers grow in holiness and resist temptation.

Modern churches that have abandoned these disciplines often struggle to help their members develop spiritual maturity beyond basic conversion and church attendance. They can lead people to faith in Christ, but they lack the spiritual resources necessary to help them grow into mature disciples.

Moral Clarity and Cultural Resistance

The Catholic Church's willingness to maintain unpopular moral positions despite cultural pressure appeals to believers who are tired of churches that modify their teaching based on public opinion polls. Catholic teaching on sexual morality, abortion, and social justice remains consistent regardless of cultural trends.

This moral clarity provides believers with stable guidance for ethical decision-making in a culture characterized by moral relativism and constant change. Catholics don't have to wonder whether their church will change its position on fundamental moral issues based on cultural pressure.

The Catholic Church's resistance to cultural accommodation also demonstrates that it's possible for churches to maintain biblical principles despite opposition from secular society. This resistance provides hope for believers who have watched their churches surrender to cultural pressure on issue after issue.

The Catholic Church's global perspective also provides balance to the American cultural captivity that characterizes many churches. Catholic social teaching draws from natural law philosophy and global experience rather than just American political categories.

BUILDING FAITHFUL COMMUNITIES

For believers who cannot find existing churches that meet their spiritual needs, the alternative is building new communities that prioritize biblical faithfulness over cultural accommodation. This building requires vision, commitment, and willingness to start small while trusting God for growth.

House Churches and Small Groups

Many faithful believers have found spiritual nourishment in house churches and small groups that focus on Bible study, prayer, and mutual accountability rather than entertainment or social activities. These smaller communities can provide the personal relationships and spiritual depth that megachurches cannot offer.

House churches allow for more participatory worship where members can share spiritual gifts, discuss Scripture, and pray for one another's needs. They also provide natural opportunities for church discipline and spiritual accountability that larger churches often lack.

The early church model described in Acts 2:42-47 provides guidance for these smaller communities: "They devoted themselves to the apostles' teaching and to fellowship, to the breaking of bread and to prayer." This devotion to essential Christian practices can be maintained more easily in smaller groups than in large congregations.

Small communities also provide opportunities for believers to develop leadership skills and spiritual maturity that might be overlooked in larger churches dominated by professional staff. Members can take turns teaching, leading worship, and providing pastoral care for one another.

Classical Christian Education

Faithful Christian communities must prioritize the education of their children in biblical truth and classical learning rather than surrendering them to secular educational systems that actively undermine Christian faith and values. This education should integrate biblical worldview with academic excellence.

Classical Christian education emphasizes the trivium - grammar, logic, and rhetoric - that develops students' ability to think clearly, communicate effectively, and evaluate arguments critically. This educational approach produces students who can defend their faith intellectually and resist cultural indoctrination.

Christian communities should also emphasize the importance of biblical literacy, ensuring that children learn Scripture thoroughly rather than just Bible stories and moral lessons. Students should be able to navigate the Bible confidently and apply its teaching to contemporary issues.

The goal of Christian education isn't just academic achievement but spiritual formation that produces young people who love God, understand his truth, and are committed to living according to his standards regardless of cultural pressure.

Intentional Community and Mutual Support

Faithful Christian communities should develop patterns of mutual support that extend beyond Sunday worship to include practical assistance, financial help, and emotional encouragement during difficult times. This support should reflect the early church's commitment to sharing resources and caring for one another's needs.

This mutual support requires intentional relationship-building that goes beyond casual church attendance to include regular fellowship, shared meals, and involvement in one another's lives. Members should know each other well enough to provide meaningful help and accountability.

Christian communities should also develop alternative economic structures that reduce dependence on secular systems and provide opportunities for members to support one another financially. This might include cooperative businesses, shared resources, and mutual aid societies.

The goal isn't isolation from the broader culture but the development of Christian community strong enough to resist cultural pressure while engaging the world with Gospel truth and Christian love.

THE COST OF FAITHFULNESS

Building or joining faithful Christian communities requires acknowledging the cost of faithfulness in a culture that is increasingly hostile to biblical Christianity. This cost includes social isolation, economic disadvantage, and potential persecution from both secular society and compromised churches.

Social Isolation and Family Pressure

Believers who choose faithful churches over popular ones often face criticism from family members and friends who don't understand why they would leave comfortable, entertaining churches for more demanding alternatives. This criticism can be particularly painful when it comes from other Christians who view faithfulness as extremism.

The social cost of faithfulness also includes reduced opportunities for networking, business relationships, and social advancement that often come through membership in popular churches. Faithful believers may find themselves excluded from social circles and professional opportunities because of their church choices.

This isolation can be especially difficult for young people who want to fit in with their peers but find themselves in churches that emphasize different values and practices than their friends' churches.

Parents must be prepared to help their children understand why faithfulness is worth the social cost.

The solution isn't to minimize this cost but to count it as part of the price of discipleship that Christ warned his followers to expect. The fellowship of faithful believers can provide community that compensates for the social isolation that faithfulness sometimes requires.

Economic and Professional Consequences

Faithful Christianity often conflicts with the economic and professional demands of contemporary American culture. Believers who prioritize church attendance, family time, and Christian service may find themselves at disadvantage in careers that demand total commitment to worldly success.

Christian business owners who operate according to biblical principles may find themselves at competitive disadvantage compared to businesses that prioritize profit over principle. This disadvantage can be particularly challenging in industries where unethical practices are common or expected.

The prosperity gospel's false promises have conditioned many Christians to expect that faithfulness will lead to material blessing, making the economic cost of faithfulness particularly difficult to accept. Faithful believers must understand that following Christ may lead to material sacrifice rather than material prosperity.

The solution isn't to abandon biblical principles for economic advantage but to trust God's provision while living according to his standards. Christian communities can help by supporting businesses that operate according to biblical principles and providing mutual aid when faithfulness results in economic hardship.

Persecution and Opposition

Faithful Christian communities should expect increasing persecution and opposition from secular authorities and cultural institutions that view biblical Christianity as a threat to their agenda. This persecution may include legal challenges, economic pressure, and social ostracism.

The persecution may also come from within Christianity as

compromised churches and denominations view faithful believers as obstacles to their accommodation with secular culture. Faithful believers may find themselves criticized and excluded by other Christians who have embraced cultural accommodation.

This persecution isn't a sign that faithful believers are doing something wrong - it's a sign that they're doing something right. Christ promised that his followers would be hated by the world, and the absence of persecution may indicate accommodation rather than faithfulness.

The solution isn't to avoid persecution but to prepare for it through spiritual discipline, community support, and commitment to biblical truth regardless of consequences. The early church's example demonstrates that persecution often strengthens rather than weakens faithful Christian communities.

CONCLUSION: THE NARROW GATE AND FEW WHO FIND IT

Christ's warning about the narrow gate that leads to life remains as relevant today as it was two thousand years ago: "Enter through the narrow gate. For wide is the gate and broad is the road that leads to destruction, and many enter through it. But small is the gate and narrow the road that leads to life, and only a few find it" (Matthew 7:13-14).

The broad road of contemporary American Christianity - with its entertainment worship, therapeutic preaching, and cultural accommodation - attracts many because it requires little sacrifice and promises much comfort. But this road leads to spiritual destruction rather than eternal life.

The narrow gate of faithful Christianity with its demanding discipleship, costly obedience, and separation from worldly values - attracts few because it requires everything and promises persecution. But this gate leads to authentic relationship with God and eternal significance.

The remnant of faithful believers exists, scattered across denominational lines and gathered in small communities that prioritize truth over comfort, transformation over entertainment, and eternal reward over temporal success. Finding these communities requires discernment, courage, and willingness to pay the cost of faithfulness.

The Jubilee Year 2025 provides a unique opportunity for believers to examine what authentic Christianity looks like and where it can be found. Whether that examination leads to Catholic conversion, faithful communities, or new expressions of biblical Christianity, the goal remains the same: following Christ faithfully regardless of cultural pressure or personal cost.

The choice is clear but not easy: the comfortable deception of popular Christianity or the challenging truth of biblical faithfulness. The broad road or the narrow gate. The many who are deceived or the few who find life.

10

THE CALL TO REFORMATION

THE EVIDENCE IS OVERWHELMING AND UNDENIABLE: AMERICAN Christianity or Churchianity has been systematically corrupted by ideologies that are fundamentally hostile to the Gospel of Jesus Christ. What began as legitimate concerns about social issues and cultural relevance has metastasized into a complete abandonment of biblical Christianity in favor of secular activism dressed in religious language.

This isn't a minor theological disagreement or a matter of denominational preference. This is spiritual warfare for the soul of Christianity itself. The enemy has infiltrated the church not through obvious attacks from outside but through subtle deceptions from within, using Christian compassion and biblical vocabulary to advance anti-Christian goals.

The transformation has been so complete that millions of Americans who consider themselves Christians have never actually heard the Gospel. They've been fed a steady diet of social justice activism, therapeutic self-help, and prosperity gospel promises while remaining ignorant of the biblical truths that could actually save their souls and transform their lives.

The stakes couldn't be higher. Entire generations are being raised in churches that teach them to see themselves primarily through racial categories rather than as children of God, to pursue material prosperity rather than spiritual holiness, and to seek political solutions rather than spiritual transformation. These false gospels don't just fail to save - they actively damn by providing false assurance while leading people away from authentic faith.

THE SYSTEMATIC CORRUPTION OF AMERICAN CHRISTIANITY

The corruption we've documented throughout this book didn't happen overnight or by accident. It represents a systematic campaign to transform Christianity from a supernatural religion focused on eternal salvation into a natural philosophy focused on temporal concerns.

The Social Justice Trojan Horse

The infiltration began with social justice ideology that exploited Christian compassion to advance Marxist goals. Well-meaning Christians were told that concern for the poor and oppressed required adoption of secular analytical frameworks that reduced all human relationships to power struggles between oppressor and oppressed groups.

This ideology didn't just add social concerns to Christian faith - it replaced Christian categories with secular ones. Instead of seeing all people as sinners in need of salvation, Christians were taught to see people as members of oppressor or oppressed groups. Instead of pursuing reconciliation through the Gospel, they were encouraged to pursue political liberation through activism.

The theological corruption was profound and comprehensive. Individual responsibility was replaced with collective guilt. Personal repentance was replaced with systemic change. Spiritual transformation was replaced with political revolution. The Gospel itself was replaced with secular ideology that promised earthly paradise through human effort.

Churches that embraced this ideology inevitably abandoned their primary mission of proclaiming the Gospel for the salvation of souls. They became political organizations using Christian resources to advance secular goals, community centers providing social services, or therapy groups helping people feel better about themselves.

The Entertainment Industrial Complex

Simultaneously, American churches embraced entertainment models that transformed worship from encounter with the holy God into consumer experiences designed to attract and retain audiences. This transformation reflected the same consumer mentality that reduced congregants to customers whose preferences must be accommodated.

The entertainment model eliminated the transcendence, reverence, and spiritual challenge that characterize authentic worship. Churches became concert venues with religious themes, motivational seminars with biblical vocabulary, or social clubs with Christian branding.

This approach attracted crowds by telling people what they wanted to hear while avoiding what they needed to hear. Sermons focused on personal fulfillment rather than personal holiness, temporal success rather than eternal significance, and emotional comfort rather than spiritual transformation.

The result was churches filled with people who had been entertained, motivated, and affirmed but never convicted, challenged, or transformed. They knew how to consume religious products but not how to follow Jesus Christ.

The Prosperity Gospel Poison

The prosperity gospel completed the corruption by promising that God wanted all believers to be healthy, wealthy, and successful in this life. This false gospel appealed to American materialism while contradicting everything Christ taught about discipleship, suffering, and the cost of following him.

Prosperity teaching transformed faith from trust in God's character into a technique for manipulating God to provide material blessings. It reduced prayer from communion with the Creator to demands for consumer goods. It turned churches into fundraising operations that enriched false teachers while impoverishing their followers.

The prosperity gospel also created a theology of victim-blaming that made suffering evidence of spiritual failure rather than normal Christian experience. Believers who experienced illness, poverty, or tragedy were told they lacked faith rather than receiving comfort and support during difficult times.

This false gospel produced shallow, materialistic believers who evaluated God's love based on their circumstances and abandoned faith when the promised blessings failed to materialize.

THE WARNING SIGNS WE CANNOT IGNORE

The six warning signs we identified provide clear indicators that churches have been compromised by these corrupting influences. These signs aren't subtle theological differences but obvious departures from biblical Christianity that any informed believer can recognize.

Women in Pastoral Leadership

Churches that ordain women pastors have demonstrated their willingness to reject clear biblical teaching in favor of cultural pressure. This compromise signals that they will abandon any biblical principle that conflicts with contemporary sensibilities.

The biblical prohibition against women in pastoral authority isn't cultural accommodation but divine design based on creation order and the nature of spiritual authority. Churches that ignore this teaching have chosen cultural acceptance over biblical obedience.

Cherry-Picking Scripture

Churches that consistently avoid difficult biblical passages while emphasizing feel-good verses have abandoned their responsibility to preach the whole counsel of God. This selective approach produces believers who know nothing about sin, judgment, or the cost of discipleship.

The "attractive gospel" that focuses only on God's love while ignoring his wrath, only on blessing while ignoring suffering, and only on comfort while ignoring challenge creates false converts who have never heard the real Gospel.

Corporate Branding Over Biblical Substance

Churches that replace detailed theological statements with meaningless marketing slogans have adopted consumer mentalities that treat congregants like customers rather than disciples. This approach prioritizes numerical growth over spiritual depth.

The abandonment of substantial doctrinal statements for catchy branding reveals churches that are more concerned with market appeal than biblical faithfulness.

Racial Obsession Over Gospel Unity

Churches that focus obsessively on race and racism have abandoned the Gospel's message of unity in Christ for secular ideologies that perpetuate division and grievance. This focus contradicts biblical teaching about spiritual identity and Christian fellowship.

The racial obsession typically serves as a gateway to other social justice causes that transform churches into political organizations rather than spiritual communities.

Authoritarian Leadership

Churches where pastors refuse to engage in biblical discussion with congregants have abandoned the biblical model of elder accountability and congregational involvement in doctrinal matters. This authoritarianism prevents the accountability that keeps churches faithful to Scripture.

Pastors who avoid scriptural discussion typically do so because they know their positions cannot be defended biblically. This avoidance signals theological compromise and pastoral cowardice.

Digital Worship Over Physical Fellowship

Churches that prioritize online engagement over physical community have misunderstood the nature of the church as the body of Christ. Virtual connection cannot replace the embodied relationships that God designed for his people.

The emphasis on digital metrics over spiritual fruit reveals churches that have adopted entertainment industry standards rather than biblical measures of success.

THE GENERATIONAL DESTRUCTION

The false teachings we've examined don't just affect individual believers - they destroy families and corrupt entire generations with lies about God, salvation, and Christian living.

The Generational Sin Heresy

The false doctrine of generational sin has been weaponized to create racial guilt and justify social justice demands. This teaching contradicts clear biblical principles of individual responsibility while undermining the sufficiency of Christ's atonement.

Churches that promote generational sin doctrine inevitably drift toward either prosperity gospel manipulation or social justice activism because the underlying theology supports both applications.

The Prosperity Gospel's Family Destruction

Prosperity teaching destroys families by creating false expectations about God's promises and material blessing. Children raised on prosperity gospel lies often abandon faith entirely when reality contradicts the false promises they were taught.

The prosperity gospel also creates tremendous financial pressure on families who are encouraged to give money they cannot afford based on false promises of miraculous returns.

The Sexual Purity Abandonment

Churches that refuse to address sexual sin have left their congregations defenseless against the hypersexualized culture that surrounds them. This pastoral failure has contributed directly to the collapse of Christian marriage and the corruption of Christian young people.

The silence on sexual issues represents one of the greatest pastoral failures in Christian history, leaving believers without biblical guidance for the most challenging moral issues of their time.

THE CATHOLIC ALTERNATIVE

Throughout this examination, the Catholic Church has emerged as the institution that has best preserved authentic Christian worship, teaching, and community life. While churches have chased cultural trends and modified their practices to maintain popularity, the Catholic Church has maintained its commitment to ancient truth and traditional practices.

The Catholic Church's preservation of sacramental life, apostolic succession, and doctrinal stability provides what churches have abandoned: historical continuity, spiritual depth, and resistance to cultural accommodation.

The conversion of young people to Catholicism reveals their hunger for authenticity in a culture saturated with artificial experiences. They're drawn to liturgy that connects them to centuries of Christian tradition, teaching that remains consistent despite cultural pressure, and worship that focuses on God rather than human entertainment.

This doesn't necessarily mean that all faithful Christians must convert to Catholicism, but it does mean that churches must learn from Catholic preservation of Christian tradition if they want to recover authentic Christianity.

THE REMNANT'S RESPONSIBILITY

For believers who recognize the corruption we've documented, the responsibility is clear: separate from compromised churches, seek authentic Christian community, and protect your families from false teaching that masquerades as Christianity.

The Necessity of Separation

Christ's call to be "in the world but not of the world" applies directly to the church situation we face today. Believers cannot remain in churches that actively promote false gospels while claiming to serve Christ faithfully.

The separation isn't schismatic but necessary - faithful believers must choose between comfortable deception and challenging truth, between popular acceptance and biblical faithfulness, between the broad road that leads to destruction and the narrow gate that leads to life.

The Search for Authentic Community

Faithful believers must seek churches that maintain biblical authority, practice church discipline, celebrate the sacraments reverently, and focus on spiritual transformation rather than entertainment or social activism.

This search may require leaving familiar churches, traveling greater distances, or even starting new communities that prioritize biblical faithfulness over cultural accommodation.

The Protection of Families

Parents have the primary responsibility to protect their children from false teaching and provide them with authentic Christian education that builds biblical worldview and spiritual maturity.

This protection requires active engagement with children's spiritual development, careful evaluation of church and school influences, and willingness to make sacrificial choices that prioritize spiritual health over social acceptance.

THE FINAL CHOICE

The choice before American Christians is stark and unavoidable: Will you choose the comfortable deception of modern Churchianity or the challenging truth of biblical Christianity? Will you follow the crowd down the broad road of cultural accommodation or walk the narrow path of faithful discipleship?

The evidence is clear. The warning signs are obvious. The consequences are eternal. The time for comfortable compromise has ended. The time for faithful courage has come.

Churchianity promises everything the world wants to hear while delivering nothing the soul actually needs. Biblical Christianity promises persecution, suffering, and the hatred of the world while delivering transformation, purpose, and eternal life with God.

The false gospels of social justice, entertainment Christianity, and prosperity teaching offer temporary comfort while leading to eternal destruction. The true Gospel of Jesus Christ offers present challenge while leading to eternal glory.

The Stakes

Souls are being lost to false gospels that promise salvation without repentance, blessing without obedience, and heaven without holiness. Families are being destroyed by teachings that contradict God's design for marriage, sexuality, and child-rearing. Entire generations are being raised on spiritual junk food that leaves them malnourished and vulnerable to every error of doctrine.

The church's witness to the world is being destroyed by institutions that look like churches but function like social clubs, entertainment venues, or political organizations. The Gospel itself is being obscured by false teachings that use Christian vocabulary while promoting anti-Christian values.

The Hope

But there is hope. Throughout history, God has preserved a remnant of faithful believers who maintain biblical truth despite cultural pressure and institutional corruption. This remnant exists today in churches that have resisted compromise, families that have maintained biblical values, and individuals who have chosen faithfulness over popularity.

The Jubilee Year 2025 provides a unique opportunity for spiritual renewal and return to authentic Christianity. Whether through Catholic conversion, faithful communities, or new expressions of biblical faith, believers can find the spiritual nourishment they've been missing in compromised churches.

The gates of hell will not prevail against Christ's true church, even when they've conquered much of institutional Christianity. The question isn't whether faithful Christianity will survive - Christ has guaranteed that it will. The question is whether you and your family will be part of the faithful remnant or part of the compromised majority.

The Call

This book is a call to a reformation that transforms individual hearts and families. It's a call to abandon the false gospels that have corrupted American Christianity and return to the authentic faith that has sustained believers for two millennia.

It's a call to choose truth over comfort, faithfulness over popularity, and eternal significance over temporal success. It's a call to take up your cross daily and follow Christ, regardless of the cost and regardless of who follows with you.

The broad road of Churchianity is crowded with people who think they're following Jesus while actually following the world. The narrow gate of biblical Christianity is traveled by few because it requires everything and promises persecution.

But it's the only path that leads to life.

APPENDIX 1

My Original Letter Of Admonishment To My Church's Leadership Over Social Justice Initiatives

I publish the following not as a means by which to shame specific people publicly, as they have already received this and it is my hope and prayer their hearts will open to the gospel and turn away from the world, but as a guideline for those who are dealing with similar situations with their churches turning to the religion of this world, the false teaching of social justice, that you may have these scriptures and arguments at your disposal to be able to right the ships in the instances where you have the power to be heard, or to burn the ships as you need to make known why you and your family must leave the places of heretical teachings.

Dear CPC Leadership Team:

My family and several others have seen many warning signs that CPC Church has become inverted to its purpose over the last year or more, in that its primary focus has shifted to how the church appears to the world, rather than rebuking the evil of the world and presenting a different way of living that is apart from the world as we are commanded. This has been a common problem with churches, especially in the United States of America, where broadcasting certain held beliefs in what many refer to as "social justice", a philosophy that has no basis in Biblical truth or the Gospel of Jesus Christ, have become a symbol of status among elites and among upper-class social circles.

The sermon Sunday, June 21st started out as something promising, speaking against false teachings straight from the word of St. Paul, but the tone of the sermon took a quick turn after the point of "do not ADD to the word", which is solid and true advice, but when elaborating on "do not detract from the word," it went into a segment where it was not scriptural, based on Christ's teachings, nor anything God has shown to us through natural order or law, but completely based on current events and current left-wing political agendas which are getting heated due to the 2020 presidential election.

The sermon was a culmination of the church choosing the prince of this world over the teachings and faith in Jesus Christ and presents a dangerous and near-Satanic vision for the future of CPC. I will elaborate on why this weekend's sermon is anti-Biblical, and therefore anti-Christ and evil, though the trend and pattern of worldly concern is not solely because of this single sermon, but a path CPC's been sliding along. The sermon of this weekend is the line where it must be rebuked as preaching false-doctrine is a slide too far into wickedness.

First, we will need to define a few terms:

1. Social Justice – a social philosophy based on liberation from "oppression", of which the latter word is defined through postmodern critical theory, specifically "forms of authority and injustice that accompanied the evolution of industrial and corporate capitalism as a political-economic system", representing primarily those who identify as a "progressive" political ideology.

2. Racism – Any conscious or unconscious bias, preference, or prejudice based on race, and in postmodern social justice terms, also including end results of socio-economic outcomes of averages of situations with non-white races, regardless of intent. In modern arguments, "racism" and "systemic racism" can go so far as to mean community solidarity.

3. BLM – a radical left-wing organization that organizes protests

and riots throughout the United States and the rest of the world with the objective of removing President Trump from office and creating anarchist societies within major metropolitan areas through the removal of police.

The Global Socio-Political Situation:

It's impossible to discuss the topics at hand without the global socio-political situation, whereas a populace who was told to quarantine for 3 months because of the virus COVID-19, in essence, imprisoned and disconnected from each other as a community – already putting us into a godless and unholy state, being one of no connection and of no hope. People have lost jobs, they've been cooped up, misery has triumphed, and this, I believe is the will of Satan to break the spirits of humanity to ripen his yield for strife, division, and violence. Without this situation, one where we are all on social media constantly, attached to "the news" – which we know at this point is sensationalist falsehoods we commonly refer to as "fake news" in order to get us agitated and act in a constant state of anger.

The church has over the course of this crisis already put too great an emphasis on the social media realm as it's transitioned to livestreams, obsessing over multiple takes, revisions, etc., rather than letting the Spirit flow naturally through live interaction and stream of consciousness. The focus has changed to one of performance and appearance rather than one of prayer and reflection. This shifts the mindset of the church from one where we are pruning branches for our sanctification as life of believers, to one of attempting to gain "likes" and focus on metrics. This has been mentioned by Pastor Scott in frustration in sermons with talk of attendance/views going down, and likewise, monetary giving going down. I know from being around church leadership that this attitude is not new, but something whispered regularly amongst the staff.

Viewing humans as metrics is a secular way of looking at humans as product consumers, rather than as creations in the image of God. In essence, numbers don't matter, only truth matters. Christ's main concern in his ministry was never the multitudes giving him views nor money, nor growing a lukewarm flock for numbers' sake, but rather He would speak unpopular truths against the mainstream culture in order to cull the flock to those who truly believed. As He stated in Matt. 7:14: "small is the gate and narrow the road that leads to life, and only a few find it." Likewise, He followed the statement, as is a common theme across Scripture to "look out for false prophets," and gave us a way to determine false prophets via their fruits. This ties into the overall socio-political situation, as we can pull back and look into the global big picture, and whether we should be supporting and condemning such actions of these socio-political movements as a church.

On False Prophecies and Messages

The church and its prophets must stay on message to the Word's truths that: the way to enlightenment is slim, indeed there is only ONE way (John 4:16), and that we should "not conform to the world" (Romans 12:2) because the world is inherently fallen. It is the devil's domain, and trying to appeal to the world is a hubris and a sign of false prophets, they and the world are apart from God.

Being set apart from the world is spoken of so often in the Bible, it seems to be one of the most important and difficult to attain tenets of the faith, otherwise, God wouldn't drill it into our heads over and over again, telling us not to be unequally yoked with unbelievers (2 Cor 6:14). We must be set apart from them, as we are chosen to be so, and this is how we display leadership and our difference to the world.

Over the past two weeks, every major news organization, every major corporation, every academic institution, every media, and entertainment outlet, have all repeated one same message, religious in the way they present it, which is "Black Lives Matter" and "racism is evil!"

You'll notice in the world's secular messages there are no specifics, there is no hope to be better in any tangible way, it's just an endless, nihilistic chant into the void that there is this phantom "bad" going on, and everyone is somehow unanimously opposed to it, yet somehow there are so many victims it's staggering (again without specifics), and all white people as a race are inherently guilty somehow of this neo-original sin.

It's easy to see what fruits are borne of this message, which is rioting, looting, violence, hatred between men, destabilization, and destruction. These fruits are not good, as they are the absence and opposite of the fruits of the Spirit: "love, joy, peace, patience, kindness, goodness, faithfulness, gentleness, and especially self-control."

Therefore, we know two facts of this "anti-racism" BLM movement: 1. The entire secular, fallen world is in chorus speaking for it and cheering it on 2. It bears fruits of devilry.

By those factors alone, the church and God's people should be unequivocally against it. When these fruits are advocated for on the pulpit, the church is bearing false witness.

The prophets speaking these words are easily identifiable as wolves in sheep's clothing, addressing another warning Christ gave us. They use the words "Black Lives Matter", "anti-fascism", and "anti-racism" because it makes it seem to any reasonable person that they couldn't disagree with it. Who in their right minds would want to say black lives don't matter? No one, and no one has, which starts to peel back the onion and the wolves' natures involved in this false witness movement.

Social Justice As Secular Religion

The devil has been attacking the Church for a long time, stripping us of cultural power, relevancy (which is a trap in and of itself for us to conform to the world and further water-down the church), and any say in society. But this is okay, to be expected, and rejoiced over, as our Master said to us: "If the world hates you, keep in mind that it hated me first." (John 15:18) If we are hated by the secular, we are likely on the right path.

The false witness being borne here is therefore another path which is being brought upon the world. This is where Social Justice becomes its own religion in essence as a philosophy devoid of religion. It exhibits the same qualities as many religions: trying to service the same human needs as a real religion while masquerading as a cause.

The social justice cause under the banner of BLM and its neo-Babel globalist funding agents, exhibits control over a group of humans, organizes them for their religious ceremonies (protests/riots), by creating a moral communal tribe by which they have to signal their virtue to one another. This again is an antithesis of Christianity, where Christ calls on us to display humility and not to broadcast our virtues to the world. Christ clearly states, "Be careful not to practice your righteousness in front of others to be seen by them. If you do, you will have no reward from your Father in heaven," (Matthew 6:1).

The Social Justice religion tribe in the last several weeks has forced people to come out and state words "Black Lives Matter" – and there have been instances where events, companies, and people have been canceled because they didn't say that exact phrase like a litany or prayer, even when they were virtue signaling about their "anti-racism" in other ways.

Real people have been hurt with lost jobs and ostracization because of a showing a lack of faith in this secular religion, again to reiterate, an evil fruit which is sewing bad crops in creating hatred in violence. In fact, those preaching anti-racism often seem the most bigoted about the topic and rigid in their religiosity in regards to social justice, another indicator of idol worship.

These are signs that not only is CPC repeating a false witness of the world, but actively diminishing the purpose of the church in giving credence to a different moral arbiter other than scripture of God, ceding it to a secular religious cult which is creating new sins and doctrine – exactly the kind of false teaching that Pastor Scott opened his message warning against at the beginning of the message. This stems from adding to the Word where it does not need to be added to.

Racism Is Not A Sin

When we get to the core of Pastor Scott's teaching this weekend, it in and of itself is unbiblical in nature, and merely based on social pressure from the above religious cult to say what sounds like a good truism on the surface (racism is bad), but when we drill into the truism, we are repeating messaging which has nothing to do with the good news of Jesus Christ nor God's will.

The following is going to be unsettling, but I specifically defined racism in the way that's meant when we speak of it in society in general, as these social justice movements like to use it as a "catch-all" term to conflate normal behavior with real problems. No one at all is defending lynching, TV and movie-style representation of beatings and abuse, nor Nazi-gas chambers. Those are not "racism" in the sense it's been defined by Pastor Scott's message, but those examples are aggressive violence, which, no matter their motive or thought behind it, is quite obviously a sin.

By the modern use of the term racism, we mean the preference for or prejudice against another race in any sense, conscious or subconscious. Ironically, in focusing on "white privilege" and "white fragility" and calling out whites as a race, Pastor Scott clearly displayed racism on the pulpit against the Caucasian race while decrying the philosophy, as "fragility" of a specific race is a negative quality inherent to said race, and therefore a negative prejudice based on race.

Logical conundrums in the message aside, the word racism has been so nebulous as used in recent weeks by the secular media which has influenced this message, and it's done to confuse and befuddle the population with the intent of bringing about demonic energies to our society. Especially when coupled with the word "systemic" as mentioned above, the word itself becomes something near meaningless, almost in taking a definition of "action I don't like or makes me angry".

Much of what's accused of racism is truly simply community solidarity around like-willed people, of which there is nothing wrong with such solidarity when it comes from a place of charity and love, and can be a positive thing, of which God demonstrates multiple times in His own solidarity or "racism" in many points of the Bible.

In St. Peter's first Epistle he speaks specifically to his Jewish congregation's community solidarity, or racism as it would be referred to in common vernacular, in regards to Gentiles (emphases mine): "But you are a chosen race, a royal priesthood, a holy nation, a people for his own possession, that you may proclaim the excellencies of him who called you out of darkness into his marvelous light." (1 Peter 2:9), where the context is Peter speaking to the Jewish Christians about God's racial preference of them over others. He further elaborates the context by telling the intended audience of the letter how to act around Gentiles or the non-chosen people: "Keep your conduct among the Gentiles honorable, so that when they speak against you as evildoers, they may see your good deeds and glorify God on the day of visitation." (1 Peter 2:12)

But in case St. Peter may have written fallible words or been misconstrued, we can turn to Christ's own ministry in how he handled and preferred the Jewish race over others:

He entered a house and did not want anyone to know it; yet he could not keep his presence secret. 5In fact, as soon as she heard about him, a woman whose little daughter was possessed by an impure spirit came and fell at his feet. 26 The woman was a Greek, born in Syrian Phoenicia. She begged Jesus to drive the demon out of her daughter.

"First let the children eat all they want," he told her, "for it is not right to take the children's bread and toss it to the dogs."

"Lord," she replied, "even the dogs under the table eat the children's crumbs."

Then he told her, "For such a reply, you may go; the demon has left your daughter."

Jesus refused a miracle to a woman because she was a non-Jew, and was so insensitive to the concept of racism that he referred to her race as DOGS when referring to the Jews preferably as Children (which is of greater importance because children have inheritance rights in the culture). This is under no uncertain terms a wildly racist statement, and the woman actually did the right thing and accepted her place and humbled herself before him, and so he took pity on her.

We are supposed to have pity and compassion for everyone, but we are also clearly supposed to prioritize our deeds and concerns based on community solidarity. God prioritized his miracles and his chosen people by race countless times across the Bible, which is not to say we should do so in every instance, as we have been given the gift of discernment depending on situations, but it does demonstrate clearly that God himself, Christ, has and does display "racism", even after the New Covenant, in the manner in which Pastor Scott condemned the philosophy.

Since God has in many instances displayed what we refer to as racism, God is infallible by nature, and God cannot by definition sin, it follows logically that racism is NOT a sin, NOT evil, and therefore should not be preached about as such from the pulpit, as it is an indication of "adding to the gospel" which was aptly warned about in Galatians.

Moreover, nowhere in the Bible does it state we are to admonish people based on their race (i.e. white privilege / white fragility / etc), as Jesus never speaks to such matters, nor do the apostles. In fact, it specifically states quite the opposite, in that we SHOULD be blind about such matters, as "There is neither Jew nor Gentile, neither slave nor free, nor is there male and female, for you are all one in Christ Jesus." There is no "white fragility" in "not seeing nor discussing racism", as implied by Pastor Scott's message and the push of the secular book he implored the congregation to read to feel guilt over the majority's own race. It sets us apart from the world to be above such matters, and we should always demonstrate love to our brothers and sisters in Christ.

Preaching In Favor of BLM and "Anti-Racism" Is Evil

Above, I've argued that BLM is a subset of a social justice modern religion, with its own services, in service of the world, amplified by worldly institutions of all stripes, and none of its leadership nor major messages have anything to do with the Gospel or Truth. It is an anti-Truth, and anything which is an anti-Truth is leading people astray from God.

Racism is also not something which is inherently a sin, even necessarily a precursor to sin, and nor should it be called one. There are real, tangible sins to which many of us in the congregation suffer from and struggle with which do not get preached upon with any regularity (chastity, abortion, adultery, sloth, greed), which is shameful by itself. Making up new sins which didn't exist in Biblical terms is not in our purview, but is something reserved by God. Since God is unchanging, he will not be creating new sins any time soon. He warns us on this in

Isaiah: "Woe to those who call evil good and good evil, who put darkness for light and light for darkness, who put bitter for sweet and sweet for bitter."

Moreover, the inappropriateness of using Father's Day, a day in which we should be encouraging fathers to be good leaders to the young and raise children in the faith, by accusing the congregation of racism, is off the charts tone-deaf for leadership to have let through in the messaging. It is damaging to the goodwill of the church and the solidarity of the body.

There is no good in this racially divisive movement of BLM or its philosophy of social justice, of which the sole purpose is to instill fear into the populace of the United States that they will destroy everything we hold dear, injure and kill our families, threaten our livelihoods and worse unless we bend to their political will. Its interests are to tear down institutions of Christianity and remove our influence from culture. We cannot be a part of it and still be preaching the Gospel of Jesus Christ.

We can dance around the subject all day, but the BLM movement's real and stated goal (Source, BLM co-founder, Patrisse Cullors, on CNN's Jake Tapper Show June 18th, 2020), is to convince the world that President Donald J. Trump is evil and must be removed and destroyed for a Marxist and globalist revolution and new world order. We should not be advocating for them in such because that is not the purview of the church.

I will leave you with one thought. At the president's rally the other day, whereby in their fruits there was no violence, no destruction by his followers, he stated we are to be one nation UNDER God, and that we are a nation of faith and will always remain so. He professes Christ and is your brother in Christ as much as he is mine, and the hatred and absolute derangement that the wicked world displays for this man means he is onto something good. As I've said in this letter, you will know them by their fruit.

You can see the difference: those like Mr. Trump and Pence who worship the cross do not crack under the strain, but the demons screech because their master and his slaves are being defeated. In the end, we can rejoice because the Truth will always win, even if it does not do so immediately within the building of the CPC Church.

At this point, the fruit of CPC is one of calling matters which are not sins, sins, in order to further a dangerous political movement, using the platform to speak untruths to a congregation which doesn't apply to them whatsoever. I can only imagine the intent, but it appears as if it's to signal to the world "we are one of you, join us because we're just like you", and if this is the case, then CPC is doing the work of the Devil.

I do not have the power in the church to enact leadership change, which needs to be done at this point in order to right the ship, as the leadership has proven repeatedly that its concerns are more about worldly appearances than about this congregation's spiritual welfare, so I will be taking my family and leaving. We will not be influenced by false witness, nor party toward taking a knee to the Prince of this world.

Sincerely,

Jon Del Arroz

APPENDIX 2

Recommended Reading for Traditional Theology

The journey from Churchianity back to authentic Christianity requires serious theological education that goes beyond contemporary Christian bestsellers and popular devotional materials. The books listed below represent the foundational works of Christian orthodoxy that have shaped faithful believers for centuries. These authors understood that Christianity is an intellectually rigorous faith that demands careful study and deep reflection.

Unlike the shallow, entertainment-focused materials that characterize much of contemporary Christian publishing, these works challenge readers to think deeply about fundamental questions of faith, doctrine, and Christian living. They provide the theological foundation necessary to recognize and resist the false teachings that have corrupted American Christianity.

ESSENTIAL FOUNDATIONAL WORKS

Orthodoxy by G.K. Chesterton

Chesterton's masterpiece demonstrates how traditional Christian doctrine provides the most reasonable and satisfying explanation for human existence and the nature of reality. Written as an intellectual autobiography, this book shows how Chesterton discovered that orthodox Christianity answered the deepest questions of philosophy and life better than any alternative worldview. Essential reading for believers who want to understand why traditional Christian teaching has endured for two millennia while modern alternatives have proven shallow and unsatisfying.

The City of God by St. Augustine

Augustine's monumental work, written in response to the fall of Rome, provides the theological framework for understanding the relationship between earthly kingdoms and the kingdom of God. This book is particularly relevant for contemporary Christians who must navigate the tension between cultural accommodation and faithful witness. Augustine's insights into human nature, divine sovereignty, and the ultimate triumph of God's kingdom provide essential perspective for believers living in a declining civilization.

Summa Theologiae by St. Thomas Aquinas

Aquinas's systematic theology represents the pinnacle of medieval scholastic thought and remains the most comprehensive treatment of Christian doctrine ever produced. While challenging for modern readers, the Summa provides unparalleled depth on questions of God's nature, human salvation, moral theology, and the sacramental life. Serious students of theology should at least familiarize themselves with Aquinas's major arguments, particularly his Five Ways for proving God's existence and his treatment of virtue ethics.

The Catechism of the Catholic Church

The official teaching document of the Catholic Church provides the most comprehensive and systematic presentation of Christian doctrine available today. Even devout Protestant readers will benefit from understanding how the Catholic Church has preserved and articulated traditional Christian teaching on fundamental questions of faith and morals. The Catechism's treatment of the Creed, the sacraments, moral life, and prayer provides a complete theological education in accessible language.

Mere Christianity by C.S. Lewis

Lewis's classic apologetic work demonstrates how to defend essential Christian truths using reason and common experience rather than denominational arguments. Originally delivered as BBC radio talks during World War II, this book shows how traditional Christian doctrine makes sense of human moral experience and provides hope in the face of evil and suffering. Lewis's clear prose and logical arguments make this an ideal starting point for readers new to serious Christian theology.

ADDITIONAL ESSENTIAL READING

The Institutes of the Christian Religion by John Calvin

Calvin's systematic theology provides the most comprehensive presentation of Reformed doctrine and demonstrates the intellectual rigor that characterized the Reformation at its best. Even readers who disagree with Calvin's conclusions will benefit from his careful biblical exegesis and logical argumentation. This work shows what Protestant theology looked like before it was corrupted by liberalism and cultural accommodation.

On the Incarnation by St. Athanasius

This early church classic explains why the doctrine of the Incarnation - that Jesus Christ is both fully God and fully man - is essential to Christian faith and human salvation. Athanasius's clear explanation of how Christ's divine nature enables him to save humanity provides crucial understanding of the Gospel that many contemporary Christians lack. This work demonstrates the theological sophistication of the early church fathers and their commitment to doctrinal precision.

The Confessions by St. Augustine

Augustine's spiritual autobiography remains one of the most influential works in Christian literature, demonstrating how intellectual pride and moral rebellion separate humans from God while divine grace provides transformation and peace. The Confessions show what genuine conversion looks like and provide a model for honest self-examination that contrasts sharply with the therapeutic Christianity popular today.

SJWs Always Lie by Vox Day

While not a theological work, this book provides essential under-standing of the social justice warrior tactics that have infiltrated and corrupted American churches. Day's analysis of how SJW ideology operates - through narrative manipulation, institutional capture, and the destruction of anyone who opposes their agenda - explains exactly how social justice has conquered so many denominations. His three laws (SJWs always lie, SJWs always double down, and SJWs always project) provide a framework for understanding the behavior patterns of church leaders who have embraced social justice ideology. Most importantly, Day offers practical strategies for resisting SJW infiltra-tion and maintaining institutional integrity against ideological subversion. Christian readers will recognize the tactics he describes being used in their own churches and denominations, making this book essential for understanding how to protect Christian institu-tions from social justice corruption.

WHY THESE BOOKS MATTER

These works represent Christianity at its intellectual and spiritual peak, when believers understood that faith required both heart and mind, both devotion and doctrine, both personal experience and objective truth. They demonstrate that authentic Christianity has always been intellectually rigorous, morally demanding, and spiritu-ally transformative.

Contemporary Christians who have been fed a steady diet of shallow devotional materials, entertainment-focused worship, and therapeutic preaching will find these books challenging. They require careful reading, serious reflection, and often multiple read-ings to fully appreciate their insights. But this intellectual effort is precisely what contemporary Christianity lacks and desperately needs.

These authors understood that Christianity makes claims about ultimate reality that must be defended intellectually, lived out morally, and experienced spiritually. They knew that faith without understanding is vulnerable to deception, that doctrine without devotion is dead orthodoxy, and that experience without truth is mere emotion.

A WARNING ABOUT CONTEMPORARY ALTERNATIVES

Readers should be cautious about contemporary Christian books that promise easy answers, quick spiritual fixes, or accommodation with secular culture. The bestseller lists are filled with books that tell Christians what they want to hear rather than what they need to hear, that offer comfort without challenge, and that reduce Christianity to therapeutic self-help or political activism.

The authors recommended above wrote for readers who wanted to understand God's truth regardless of its difficulty or cultural unpopularity. They assumed that their readers were serious about spiritual growth and willing to invest the intellectual effort necessary for theological understanding.

Contemporary Christian publishing, by contrast, often assumes that readers want entertainment, inspiration, and validation rather than instruction, conviction, and transformation. The result is a flood of books that may make readers feel good temporarily but fail to provide the theological foundation necessary for spiritual maturity.

THE PATH FORWARD

Serious engagement with these theological classics will provide readers with the intellectual and spiritual resources necessary to recognize and resist the false teachings that have corrupted American Christianity. They will develop the theological discernment necessary to distinguish between authentic Christianity and its contemporary counterfeits.

More importantly, these books will connect readers to the great tradition of Christian thought that extends back to the apostles themselves. They will discover that they are part of a community of faith that transcends denominational boundaries, cultural differences, and historical periods.

This discovery provides both humility and confidence - humility because it reveals how much previous generations understood that contemporary Christians have forgotten, and confidence because it demonstrates that authentic Christianity has survived every challenge and will continue to do so.

The choice is clear: readers can continue consuming the spiritual junk food that characterizes contemporary Christian publishing, or they can feast on the rich theological heritage that has sustained faithful believers for centuries. The effort required for serious theological study is significant, but the rewards - intellectual satisfaction, spiritual depth, and theological discernment - are immeasurable.

These books will not make Christianity easier or more comfortable. They will make it deeper, richer, and more intellectually satisfying. They will provide the theological foundation necessary for faithful Christian living in a culture that is increasingly hostile to biblical truth.

The journey from Churchianity to Christianity requires serious theological education. These books provide the roadmap for that journey.

APPENDIX 3

Questions for Evaluating Your Church

The following questions are designed to help believers identify whether their church has been compromised by the false teachings and corrupt practices documented in this book. These questions should be asked honestly and answered based on observable evidence rather than wishful thinking or loyalty to familiar institutions.

A single "yes" answer to any of these questions indicates cause for concern. Multiple "yes" answers suggest serious compromise that may require finding a new church. Remember: your eternal soul and your family's spiritual welfare are more important than social comfort or institutional loyalty.

LEADERSHIP AND AUTHORITY QUESTIONS

Does your church have women in pastoral positions or teaching roles over men?

This includes female senior pastors, teaching pastors, or women who regularly preach to mixed adult congregations. Churches that violate the clear biblical prohibition in 1 Timothy 2:12 have demonstrated their willingness to reject Scripture when it conflicts with cultural pressure.

Does your pastor avoid discussing controversial biblical passages or difficult theological topics?

Pastors who consistently avoid preaching about sin, judgment, sexual morality, or other "uncomfortable" biblical truths have abandoned their responsibility to preach the whole counsel of God.

Is it difficult or impossible to have serious theological discussions with church leadership?

Leaders who refuse to engage in biblical dialogue about church direction or doctrinal concerns are operating more like corporate executives than biblical shepherds.

Does your church leadership change theological positions based on cultural trends?

Churches that modify their teaching on marriage, sexuality, gender roles, or other fundamental issues to accommodate cultural pressure have chosen worldly acceptance over biblical faithfulness.

Are church decisions made primarily by professional staff rather than through biblical elder leadership?

Churches that operate like corporations with CEO pastors and professional management have abandoned the biblical model of elder-led congregational governance.

WORSHIP AND SACRAMENTAL QUESTIONS

Does your church prioritize entertainment value over reverent worship?

This includes concert-style lighting, fog machines, performance-focused music, and worship that feels more like a show than an encounter with the holy God.

Is communion/the Lord's Supper treated as a rare afterthought rather than a central sacrament?

Churches that celebrate communion monthly or less frequently, or treat it as a brief symbolic ritual, have lost sight of its central importance in Christian worship.

Does your church use corporate-style slogans instead of detailed theological statements?

Marketing phrases like "Connect. Grow. Serve." or "Real People. Real Faith." indicate a consumer mentality that treats congregants like customers rather than disciples.

Is your church's worship indistinguishable from secular entertainment?

If removing explicitly Christian lyrics would make your worship service identical to a motivational seminar or concert, your church has abandoned distinctively Christian worship.

Does your church emphasize online engagement over physical fellowship?

Churches that measure success by social media metrics, livestream views, or digital engagement rather than spiritual fruit have misunderstood the nature of Christian community.

TEACHING AND DOCTRINE QUESTIONS

Does your pastor consistently preach from the same feel-good biblical passages while avoiding difficult texts?

Repeated sermons on God's love, personal fulfillment, and positive thinking while avoiding passages about sin, judgment, and the cost of discipleship indicate cherry-picking Scripture.

Does your church teach or promote prosperity gospel principles?

This includes "seed faith" offerings, promises of financial breakthrough, "name it and claim it" theology, or teaching that God wants all believers to be wealthy and healthy.

Does your church promote "generational sin" or "generational curse" teaching?

Churches that teach inherited guilt, ancestral sin patterns, or the need for special prayers to break family curses have embraced unbiblical doctrine that contradicts individual responsibility and Christ's sufficient atonement.

Are sermons primarily therapeutic rather than trans-

formative?

Messages that focus on making people feel better about themselves rather than calling them to repentance and holiness have replaced the Gospel with psychology.

Does your church avoid teaching about hell, divine judgment, or the exclusivity of salvation through Christ?

Churches that eliminate "offensive" biblical doctrines to avoid cultural criticism have abandoned essential Christian truth.

SOCIAL JUSTICE AND POLITICAL QUESTIONS

Does your church regularly address racism, white privilege, or systemic oppression from the pulpit?

Churches that make racial issues a central focus have typically embraced social justice ideology that contradicts biblical teaching about unity in Christ.

Does your church promote social justice books, workshops, or training programs?

Materials like "White Fragility," "Woke Church," or similar resources indicate that your church has been infiltrated by secular social justice ideology.

Does your church leadership take political positions on contemporary issues while claiming to be "prophetic"?

Churches that regularly address political topics while avoiding clear biblical teaching about personal sin have confused social activism with Gospel ministry.

Does your church emphasize collective guilt based on racial or cultural identity?

Teaching that requires people to confess sins they didn't commit based on their skin color or cultural background contradicts biblical principles of individual responsibility.

Does your church participate in interfaith social justice initiatives that minimize doctrinal differences?

Partnerships that prioritize political activism over Gospel truth indicate that your church values social change more than spiritual transformation.

DISCIPLESHIP AND CHRISTIAN LIVING QUESTIONS

Does your church avoid addressing sexual morality, marriage, and family issues?

Churches that refuse to teach biblical standards for sexuality, gender roles, and family structure have abandoned their pastoral responsibility to address the most destructive sins of our time.

Does your church practice church discipline for serious sin?

Churches that never remove unrepentant members or address moral failures within the congregation have abandoned the biblical mandate for maintaining holiness.

Does your church emphasize numerical growth over spiritual maturity?

Churches that measure success primarily by attendance numbers, baptisms, or budget growth rather than evidence of spiritual transformation have adopted worldly success metrics.

Does your church provide substantial biblical education or primarily offer entertainment and social activities?

Churches that focus more on fun activities than serious Bible study have prioritized attraction over spiritual development.

Does your church encourage members to engage seriously with Scripture or primarily rely on pastoral teaching?

Churches that discourage independent Bible study or theological questioning have created unhealthy dependence on human authority rather than biblical truth.

FINANCIAL AND INSTITUTIONAL QUESTIONS

Does your church operate more like a business than a spiritual community?

This includes professional marketing, customer service

approaches, brand management, and revenue-focused decision making.

Does your church leadership live lavishly while encouraging sacrificial giving from members?

Pastors with expensive homes, luxury cars, or extravagant lifestyles while preaching about generosity have adopted prosperity gospel values.

Does your church spend more money on facilities and staff than on missions and ministry?

Churches that prioritize impressive buildings and professional staff over Gospel proclamation and service to others have misplaced priorities.

Does your church use high-pressure fundraising techniques or promise spiritual benefits for financial giving?

"Seed faith" offerings, building fund campaigns with spiritual promises, or guilt-based giving appeals indicate prosperity gospel influence.

Is your church's budget and financial information kept secret from members?

Churches that refuse to provide financial transparency to their members are operating more like private businesses than accountable spiritual communities.

FAMILY AND CHILDREN QUESTIONS

Does your church's children's ministry emphasize entertainment over biblical education?

Programs that focus more on games, activities, and fun than serious Bible teaching are failing to provide children with the spiritual foundation they need.

Does your church support or accommodate LGBTQ+ ideology in any form?

Churches that affirm homosexual relationships, transgender identity, or "progressive" sexual ethics have abandoned biblical teaching about sexuality and gender.

Does your church undermine parental authority by teaching children to question their parents' values?

Programs that encourage children to embrace "social justice" values that contradict their parents' biblical convictions are dividing families rather than strengthening them.

Does your church provide resources for protecting children from cultural indoctrination?

Churches that fail to help parents address pornography, social media dangers, and secular educational influences have abandoned their responsibility to support Christian families.

Does your church promote "youth-friendly" approaches that compromise biblical standards?

Programs that avoid "controversial" biblical teachings to attract young people are failing to provide the spiritual challenge that produces mature disciples.

CONCLUSION: WHAT THE ANSWERS MEAN

If you answered "yes" to several of these questions, your church has likely been compromised by the false teachings and corrupt practices documented in this book. The more "yes" answers you have, the more serious the compromise and the more urgent your need to find authentic Christian community.

Remember that leaving a compromised church is necessary for your spiritual health and your family's protection. Christ calls his followers to be "wise as serpents" in recognizing spiritual danger and "innocent as doves" in maintaining purity from worldly corruption.

The goal isn't to find a perfect church - no such institution exists this side of heaven. The goal is to find a church that maintains biblical authority, practices authentic worship, teaches sound doctrine, and prioritizes spiritual transformation over worldly success.

Your eternal soul is worth more than social comfort, family tradition, or institutional loyalty. Choose wisely, and choose based on biblical truth rather than human preference.

The narrow gate that leads to life is traveled by few, but it's the only path worth taking.

NEWSLETTER

While this book is somewhat out of my ordinary wheelhouse as a fiction writer, you may enjoy my other writings if you enjoyed my thought processes here.

Sign up for my newsletter so you don't miss new releases and more. Get THREE FREE BOOKS for doing so!

http://www.delarroz.com/newsletter

I am also fighting the good fight as a journalist with articles on the culture, Christianity, and more at http://www.fandompulse.com

ALSO BY JON DEL ARROZ

THE NANO TEMPLAR
Read the hit Christian sci-fi series:
Justified
Sanctified
Glorified

THE ARYSHAN WAR
Read Jon Del Arroz's original space opera universe:
The Stars Entwined
The Stars Asunder
The Stars Rejoined
Colony Launch
The Roles We Play

THE ADVENTURES OF Baron Von Monocle:
Read the bestselling steampunk fantasy series:
For Steam And Country
The Blood Of Giants

The Fight For Rislandia
The Iron Wedding
The Steam Knight
The Crystal Conspiracy

THE TERRAN IMPERIUM Chronicles
Read the far future military sci-fi spy thriller series:
The Immortal Edge
Into The Black

OTHER BOOKS
The Demon's Eye

Made in the USA
Middletown, DE
16 November 2025

20646618R00109